STEWARDSHIP
and the
ECONOMY OF GOD

LIBRARY OF CHRISTIAN STEWARDSHIP

Stewardship in Contemporary Theology. T. K. Thompson, editor. New York: Association Press, 1960.

Christian Stewardship and Ecumenical Confrontation. T. K. Thompson, editor. New York: Dept. of Stewardship & Benevolence, National Council of Churches, 1961.

Stewardship in Mission. Winburn T. Thomas, editor. Englewood Cliffs: Prentice-Hall, 1964.

Handbook of Stewardship Procedures. T. K. Thompson. Englewood Cliffs: Prentice-Hall, 1964.

The Christian Meaning of Money. Otto A. Piper. Englewood Cliffs: Prentice-Hall, 1965.

Stewardship Illustrations. T. K. Thompson, editor. Englewood Cliffs: Prentice-Hall, 1965.

Stewardship in Contemporary Life. T. K. Thompson, editor. New York: Association Press, 1965.

Why People Give. Martin E. Carlson. New York: Council Press, 1968.

Punctured Preconceptions. Douglas W. Johnson and George W. Cornell. New York: Friendship Press, 1972.

The Steward: A Biblical Symbol Come of Age. Douglas John Hall. New York: Friendship Press, 1982.

Christian Mission: The Stewardship of Life in the Kingdom of Death. Douglas John Hall. New York: Friendship Press, 1985.

Teaching and Preaching Stewardship: An Anthology. Nordan C. Murphy, editor. New York: Friendship Press, 1985.

Imaging God: Dominion as Stewardship. Douglas John Hall. Grand Rapids: Eerdmans and New York: Friendship Press, 1986.

Public Theology and Political Economy: Christian Stewardship in Modern Society. Max L. Stackhouse. Grand Rapids: Eerdmans, 1987.

The Stewardship of Life in the Kingdom of Death. Douglas John Hall. Grand Rapids: Eerdmans, 1988 (revised edition of *Christian Mission*).

Stepping Stones of the Steward. Ronald E. Vallet. Grand Rapids: Eerdmans, 1989.

Stewardship and the Economy of God. John Reumann. Grand Rapids: Eerdmans and Indianapolis: The Ecumenical Center for Stewardship Studies, 1992.

*Title is out of print

STEWARDSHIP
and the
ECONOMY OF GOD

John Reumann

William B. Eerdmans Publishing Company
Grand Rapids, Michigan

The Ecumenical Center for Stewardship Studies
Indianapolis, Indiana

Copyright © 1992 by the Ecumenical Center for Stewardship Studies

Published by Wm. B. Eerdmans Publishing Co.
255 Jefferson Ave. S.E., Grand Rapids, Mich. 49503
All rights reserved

Printed in the United States of America

ISBN 0-8028-0653-8

Unless otherwise noted, the Scripture quotations in this publication are from the
Revised Standard Version of the Bible, copyrighted 1946, 1952 © 1971, 1973
by the Division of Christian Education of the National Council of Churches of
Christ in the U.S.A., and used by permission.

CONTENTS

—— FOREWORD ——

In large part, this book is based on lectures given by John Reumann in 1987 and 1988. Denominational stewardship leaders from Canada and the United States heard John's lectures at the 1987 Winter Event of the Commission on Stewardship of the National Council of Churches of Christ in the U.S.A. In 1988, theological educators from across North America gathered in Toronto at a Colloquy for Theological Educators to gain new insights about how stewardship can be incorporated into the curricula of theological schools.

John Reumann has put these and other thoughts together, presenting us with a work that is remarkably broad and encompassing in scope. The book looks particularly at the meaning of stewardship — or, more specifically, *oikonomia,* the Greek word often translated as "stewardship." Twenty years ago, he notes, the word "stewardship" was thought to have had its day. Now it is undergoing a rebirth. In the 1970s, both the word "stewardship" and the practice of stewardship went into decline in many churches. A rediscovery of the term by journalists and society in general has since elevated stewardship into a new and somewhat different prominence.

This book looks at the usage of stewardship terms and concepts that ranges from the pre-Christian Greek world to biblical use in the Old and New Testament to Greek and Latin writers to church history, including patristic, medieval, Reformation, and later developments.

He identifies and explores vantage points for reuniting stewardship and the economy of God. This is followed by an examination of three approaches to stewardship within the economy of God: stewardship and the history of salvation; stewardship, creation, and the role of all humanity within the economy of God; and the place of the apocalyptic outlook in the economy of God. Finally, he explores ways of applying the rediscovered word "stewardship" in God's economy.

Interestingly, Reumann reports that in the history of the church the word *oikonomia* has been used to refer to the Incarnation, baptism, the Transfiguration, and Jesus' death on the cross. Gregory of Nazianzus wrote that a pastor is an *oikonomos* of souls and dispenser of the word.

Reumann gives considerable attention to the writings of Douglas John Hall, who in recent years has had a significant impact on our understanding of stewardship. Three of Hall's books are part of the Library of Christian Stewardship.

This book is not one to be read once, placed on the bookshelf, and then forgotten. Rather, it will be savored and turned to as a valuable resource over many years to come.

Thank you, John Reumann.

Ronald E. Vallet
Executive Director
Ecumenical Center for Stewardship Studies

─── AUTHOR'S PREFACE ───

The wide-ranging material in this book was originally presented in lectures at the Winter Event of the Commission on Stewardship of the National Council of the Churches of Christ in the U.S.A., 1-4 December 1987, under the title "Making History: Our Role as Stewards," and at the Commission's Colloquy for Theological Educators, 6-9 July 1988, in Toronto, Canada, under the title "Stewardship in History: Past Realities, Present Context, and Future Possibilities." At the latter sessions I also gave a lecture entitled "The Tithe: Christian Bane or Blessing?" which was subsequently published in the *Journal of Stewardship* (42 [1990]: 20-29). I have reassembled these materials for this volume and series at the invitation of the Ecumenical Center for Stewardship Studies and its director, Dr. Ronald E. Vallet.

It is a pleasure for me to note the stimulation of the ecumenical fellowship at meetings of the Commission on Stewardship. Here, in a far more lively — and, I dare say, theological — way than is typically the case in denominational stewardship structures, I have found challenging new frontiers and efforts to provide the encounter among theological faculty and others that was characteristic of the stewardship movement over thirty years ago. There are few other places where process theologians and systematicians, Old and New Testament scholars, historians, practical theologians specializing in preaching, education, worship, and, yes, fund-raising, as well as church executives, laity, and pastors come together so vitally in the life of the churches.

But the pages that follow represent far more than several years of engagement with such people. They also reflect some forty years of attention to the Greek word family that gives us "steward" and "stewardship" in the New Testament and subsequent Christian usage. As a graduate student reading Ignatius of Antioch, Irenaeus, Clement of Alexandria, and Origen, I was never sure how to translate the word *oikonomia*. Intrigued by its nuances, I wrote my doctoral dissertation on it and related terms at the University of Pennsylvania Department of Classical Studies under Morton Scott Enslin, a Baptist seminary professor who read the Church Fathers in a way far different from that common among those who work in the "patristic tradition."

Since completing that work in 1957, I have continued publication on aspects of the theme, often in technical journals, from time to time. The dissertation itself was published almost in its entirety in journals edited by the Metropolitan of Aksum in Ethiopia (who later became the Archbishop of Thyateira and Great Britain). In later theology one speaks of things done *kat' oikonomian,* "by economy," or as Western Christians might say, "by dispensation," and it was argued by Archbishop Methodios that the Orthodox ought to remain active in the ecumenical movement on the grounds of such an "economy" or condescension *(sunkatabasis),* beyond what a strict doctrinal and legal interpretation required.

Writing this book thus provided me with an opportunity to return to an area long of interest, study of which was aided by a Guggenheim fellowship in 1965-66. It was nurtured by occasional elective courses at the Lutheran Theological Seminary, Philadelphia, under the rubric "Salvation History and Stewardship," as well as lectures and workshops with clergy and laity, including the African Methodist Episcopal Church in the southeastern United States at a time when segregation dominated national life in ways it did not in Christian fellowship. It has been a preoccupation of mine in recent years to collect examples of how often "stewardship" as a word has made its way back into American English after the churches gave up on the term. One vivid example turned up in the obituary of Paul Anthony Ryan in the Philadelphia *Inquirer* for 12 November 1991. Ryan was reported to have been "headmaster at Smokey Joe's — the noisy cave of a bar that former President Gerald R. Ford once called the 17th institution of higher learning at the University of Pennsylvania." Said the obituary, "under the stewardship of Mr. Ryan, Smokey Joe's was the crowded, happy, let-your-hair-down social center of campus life. . . ." The word is certifiably current journalese.

Few topics have I found to be so broadly ecumenical. It begins with a Protestant word and an American theme, "stewardship"; yet the topic is rooted in the age-old "economy of God" long dear to Eastern Orthodox, Roman Catholic, and Anglican theology and is tied linguistically and in content with "dispensationalism," a favorite concept among fundamentalists. In its secular form, the theme also proves appropriate for Jews and adherents of other world religions, as well as among nontheists and atheists. My intent here is not to define "stewardship" exhaustively or to settle how far it goes beyond fund-raising; rather, I am interested in expanding the horizons of the term so that others can make the applications in their congregations, dioceses, denominations, and councils.

May these pages stir up thinking theologically and lead to actions in church and world! There is more to stewardship than reviving the tithe through episcopal and clerical example. The stewardship enterprise is for all God's people. Today, amid financial exigencies in so many churches, thought is not always given to the ethics, let alone the theological foundations, of fund-raising. I myself have been stimulated by some of the proposals made in recent years under the banner of "stewardship" but have not hesitated to be critical of some of them on theological and historical grounds. There has all too often been a tendency to let the concerns of an age or an individual fill up the void in what a term such as "stewardship" means. This book is an effort to relate classical and cutting-edge concepts and so give substance to the enterprise.

In writing the text, I have tried to confine the apparatus of scholarship chiefly to the notes. You can consult them when you want to track down references and evidence. Occasionally I also use the notes to expand on issues or outline opportunities for further investigation. In the text proper I seek to call all readers to stewardship within their religious communities and world, set within an even broader "economy of God," so as to be stewards in life, under God's stewardship for all life.

To some of my many mentors in stewardship I dedicate these pages: my parents, the Rev. W. Paul Reumann and Ethel M. (Rauth) Reumann, who taught by preaching and example in a Lutheran parsonage; my uncle the Rev. Otto G. Reuman, a Congregationalist missionary and minister; and Dr. T. K. Thompson, man of vision in ecumenical stewardship work for the National Council of Churches, who introduced me to wider circles to show how a doctoral dissertation can relate to church life.

We are unexpectedly witnessing in secular society the rebirth of a biblical and "church" word that twenty years ago many thought had had its day. That word is "stewardship." A generation or two ago its use was widespread in Christian circles, especially among Protestants. Although the term has a relatively limited usage in the New Testament, during the 1940s, '50s, and '60s it enjoyed a wide currency among Christians in discussions of God's goodness, particularly with respect to money and other material resources. Then it went out of style, and only a few fought a rearguard action in parishes or denominations here and there to keep it in use.

But just as Christians by and large gave up on the term, somehow the world rediscovered it. Not only the environmentalists and "the green" political parties but finance, business, and government agencies too. A striking example popped up in a New York *Times* story of 19 August 1990 about the plight of Soviet farming. Near Rostov, Mr. Viktor A. Gulov, once the director of a large collective farm, had led the farm people, on the basis of what he had observed on a trip to Canada, into "self-sufficient, profit-oriented teams, called cooperatives, a step in the evolution toward real farms." Under the new system, the farmers not only earned more money but also experienced "the satisfaction and responsibility of stewardship." In this context the word denotes care for the land, responsibility for resources, and a sense of well-being about handling what was entrusted to them. There are no religious overtones, no suggestion that Christians of any sort were involved.

In the pages that follow, numerous examples will be cited from newspapers and magazines of this proliferating use of "steward" words. New interest in this old theme is arising in the churches too. But how should "stewardship" be understood? Over the years it has had many meanings. Definitions in the church, where the term has been used most extensively, fall into two categories, associated with phases through which the modern stewardship movement has passed. Most definitions below come from the second phase.

The first category of definitions stems from the early association of stewardship almost exclusively with money and fund-raising. At times it was allied with "benevolence," which made it sound a little less crass. Benevolence still involves the giving of money, but it is often directed to causes outside the local congregation and beyond parochial self-support. It raises one's vision to a wider world.

The connotations of fund-raising and benevolence associated with stewardship at least helped to establish a clear and forthright understanding of the term, for they dealt with the necessary matter of meeting (and possibly exceeding) budgets and devising equitable ways for all congregations of a denomination to share in a total budget. A striking example of this concern is evident in the title for the unit charged with stewardship in the African Methodist Episcopal Church in the early 1960s: the Department of Minimum Salary — a real issue, then or now, for impoverished preachers and church workers!

In subsequent years the stewardship movement often had great difficulty in overcoming and moving beyond this traditional association with "mere money." As a counterbalance, groups such as the Lutheran Laymen's Movement for Stewardship stressed the stewardship of the "three T's" — treasure, time, and talents — in order to get beyond the "cash-flow" image. But in trying to shape a concern for more than just fund-raising, the steward-ship movement moved into a second stage.

The second category of definitions stems from attempts that have been made more recently (at least since the 1950s and again in the last decade) to construe stewardship so broadly that it seems to encompass all of Christian life and theology. As "stewardshipologists" pushed beyond old issues such as whether to use single-pocket collection envelopes or the two- or three-pocket varieties, toward what they hoped would be a "theology of stewardship," they began to claim that *everything* in Christian belief and practice belonged under stewardship. Their concerns became as broad as systematic theology, as wide-ranging as social ethics. At times it has seemed that the students of steward-ship would produce a literature as broad in scope as Barth's *Church Dogmatics* or the *Encyclopaedia Britannica!*

Such breadth of interest may not be a bad thing. We often test an idea whose time has come by seeing how much weight its skeleton and sinews will bear, how far its framework can stretch. This same sort of proliferation of claims has also occurred with other phenomena in church life, such as the Christian education movement, the liturgical movement, and biblical theology.

To get some idea of the extent of this proliferation of claims, consider the following ways in which different leaders or groups have defined stewardship:

The word of the social gospel made flesh.
— John M. Versteeg (1923)

The *practice* of the Christian religion. It is neither a department of life nor a sphere of activity. It is the Christian conception of life as a whole, manifested in attitudes and actions.
— W. H. Greever (1937)

Human thanksgiving for divine goodness and mercy. . . . What I do after I have said: I believe.
— Clarence Stoughton (1949)

3

> Partnership with Christ, through the Holy Spirit, in following the purpose of God in the world.
>
> — A. C. Conrad (1955)

> The living expression of the total content of the Christian faith.
>
> — T. A. Kantonen (1951)

> That for which I am responsible to God for my fellow men [and hence] consecration to this task [of uniting people to the church].
>
> — T. A. Kantonen (1956)[1]

Some of these definitions might still be usable, or at least are worth discussing, although today we would rephrase some of their ideas in more inclusive language.

In 1946 the United Stewardship Council of the Churches of Christ in the United States and Canada adopted the following definition, out of 150 that were suggested:

> the practice of systematic and proportionate giving of time, abilities, and material possessions, based on the conviction that these are trusts from God to be used in his service for the benefit of all mankind in grateful acknowledgment of Christ's redeeming love.[2]

This statement was probably influential in getting the following definition for "stewardship" into *Webster's Third New International Dictionary* in 1961:

> the aspect of the religious life and church administration dealing with the individual's responsibility for sharing systematically and proportionately his time, talent, and material possessions in the service of God and for the benefit of all mankind.

A subsequent statement in 1964 from the Department of Stewardship and Benevolence of the National Council of the Churches of Christ in the U.S.A. reads thus:

4

Christian stewardship is man's grateful and obedient response to God's redeeming love, expressed by the use of all resources for the fulfillment of Christ's mission in the world.

Christian stewardship:
> Recognizes all of life as a trust from God;
> Acknowledges that man's response is powered by the Holy Spirit;
> Involves Christians individually and corporately;
> Requires responsible management of all God-given resources; and

Maintains that man should dedicate a worthy portion of his time, abilities, and money for the advancement of Christ's mission in the world through His Church.[3]

For the *Twentieth Century Encyclopedia of Religious Knowledge* in 1955 Robert Cashman provided this somewhat flamboyant definition: "one of the basic doctrines of the Christian religion . . . not merely a scheme to raise money for the church, but a means of entering actively into partnership with God. . . . Stewardship . . . is the noblest expression of the Christian ideal."[4]

Shortly thereafter, stewardship went into eclipse in the churches. It was society that resurrected the term. To grasp what it might mean today, we need to look at some of its history, from the underlying New Testament term, through its Anglo-Saxon etymology, to these modern developments of renewal.

We will begin with an examination of early Christian use of the Greek word, *oikonomia,* that gives us the term "stewardship" in the New Testament. This study also involves, of necessity, the term for "steward" *(oikonomos)* and the verb "to be a steward" *(oikonomein),* as well as related terms such as *dioikein,* "to administer." At times our exploration will take in the Latin equivalents for *oikonomia,* for these also become part of the story, especially and somewhat surprisingly through "dispensationalism" in American fundamentalism. These equivalents include the Latin nouns *dispensatio, dispositio,* and a transliteration of the

Greek into Latin, *oeconomia* — from which, in turn, came the older English spelling "oeconomics," from which we derive the modern spelling "economics." This probe will go beyond the New Testament, into Christian writers of the second to the sixth or eighth centuries. Such a step is necessary not only to suggest links to Roman Catholic, Anglican, and Eastern Orthodox thought but also because some of our most important insights will turn up from these sources. Their notion of a "divine economy" will, in particular, lead to an understanding of history that has guided Christians in various ways and dominated much of life for centuries.

This exploration into the word that can be, and sometimes is, translated "stewardship" will reveal a host of meanings and connotations, far richer than many of the most ardent stewardship advocates have ever dreamed. At the same time as this study turns up core meanings and lesser senses, it will also indicate changes that have occurred in usage and suggest some parameters or limits. These interconnections and emphases from past history may serve as clues for directions today.

In choosing this "word-study" approach to the original biblical terminology, we will avoid the trap of starting with the term "stewardship" in English Bibles.[5] That word and "steward" occur in the King James Bible some eighteen times and are even more common in the Revised Standard Version (twenty-three occurrences), though less so in the New Revised Standard Version.[6] Our English word "steward" comes from the Anglo-Saxon for a "ward" in charge of a *stigu,* or sty for pigs.[7] While "steward(ship)" thus had a humble, earthly sense, in the "sty-ward" on a pig farm, a homely sense true often to the connotations of *oikonomia* in Greek, it also lost in translation any connection to the "house" or "household" (Greek *oikos*) that the German rendering *Haushalter(schaft)* has, for example, preserved, and probably obscured any sense of "managing." "Steward" and "stewardship" introduced a new turn in the course of development this conception was to take and so laid the groundwork for the further American lines of development.

But we seek here to go back behind the "steward" translation to the original New Testament term. In so doing we can expect to find certain connections, emphases, and shifts in meaning. These can be briefly sketched in advance. See Chart I on page 8 for a visual overview and summary of the development that is outlined below.

1. *Oikonomia,* a many-faceted term that can be translated "stewardship" as well as in a variety of other ways, was "in the air" of the first-century world. It was a buzzword — as "stewardship" is again today in American English. It had an amazing host of established meanings in many areas of life. It was a word capable of new applications, a "word field" of expanding horizons. I shall sketch the chief classical and Hellenistic uses below as the basis for later usage in the New Testament and other early Christian writers. We cannot grasp these subsequent applications without some idea of the pre-Christian, pagan senses. The classical Greek uses provide the background for Christian usage.

2. A surprise: the Bible, even the New Testament, makes comparatively little use of this terminology. The Old Testament material can be dealt with quite briefly. Our attention there will be on the Greek translations of the Hebrew Scriptures, but the story is the same in both: no significant usage. For the New Testament there is a bit more evidence at which to look. This we shall take up in connection with Jesus and certain verses in the Gospels (the terms occur only in the Synoptics, not John). Then we shall turn to the theologically more significant examples in Paul and the other epistles. Some of these references are in letters unquestionably written by Paul; others are in what some call "Deutero-Pauline writings," such as Colossians and Ephesians, and in the "Pastoral Epistles" (1, 2 Timothy, Titus). One example is in 1 Peter. But even that epistle has sometimes been characterized as Pauline because of its form and ideas, or at least is characteristic of "common apostolic Christianity." Thus there is some justification for grouping these references in the epistles together.

CHART I: THE DEVELOPMENT OF THE USE OF OIKONOMIA TERMINOLOGY

Classical and Hellenistic Usages	New Testament Applications	Early Christian Writers
1. In the household (*oikos*) — *oikonomia* = management of the household; *oikonomos* = household manager. Cf. in Latin *oeconomia*, English "oeconomics," later "economics" (as in "home economics," domestic science); *dispensatio*.	1. Luke 16:1-8 (the "unjust" *oikonomos*); 1 Cor. 4:1-2, Luke 16:10-12; 12:42, "the faithful steward." →	This usage continued generally and in Christian circles.
2. In the city-state (*polis*) — *oikonomia* = management of the city-state in military, civic, societal, and even religious matters.	2. Rom. 16:23, *oikonomos* = city treasurer. →	This usage continued in both general and Christian circles.
3. In the arts, literature, history, rhetoric — *oikonomia* = arrangement of material.	(no clear examples)	Applied widely, especially by Christian historians after Augustine.
4. In the world or universe (*kosmos*) — *oikonomia* = (God's) arrangement or management of the world and its affairs.	4. 1 Cor. 4:1-2; Col. 1:25; Eph. 1:10; 3:2, 9. →	Expansion of usage, explosion into new applications.

There are not enough *oikonomia* terms in Scripture to warrant calling it a major biblical concept, but there is enough usage in the New Testament to point the way to future developments.

3. The "patristic" use — that among the Church Fathers, or, to employ inclusive language, writers in the church of the second and following centuries — will prove most significant. This classical Greek term, which was "in the air" but found little New Testament use, suddenly burst into prominence among Christians of these later centuries. The applications by such writers of *oikonomia* terms are to be understood therefore in light of two factors: (a) in many cases they reflect and pick up on earlier classical senses, and (b) for Christians they developed new linguistic applications in light of the Christ event. Patristic meanings will therefore again and again combine classical Greek backgrounds, understandable to the world of the day, and new aspects derived from the gospel of Jesus Christ.

CHAPTER I

The "Economy of God" in Scripture and Antiquity

Before taking up the biblical use of Greek "stewardship" terms, it is necessary to survey the pre-Christian development of this family of words. From them clues will come for understanding aspects of New Testament terminology and subsequent Christian theological development. In particular this will involve what came to be an almost technical term, "the economy of God," in popular philosophy and as a worldview of history, one that echoes, behind stewardship, down to today.

A. Greek Background

1. In the Household

The starting point is the Greek word *oikos*, meaning "household." The concept of the household involved not only husband and wife and children but also an "extended family," including servants and slaves. All was presided over by the "master of the household" (*oikodespotēs*, a term used in Luke 12:39; Matt. 13:27, 52; 20:1; 21:33). Originally the managing of the household was, in a typical, small household, in the hands of the wife; in a

11

larger unit, it was left in the hands of a skilled slave or freedman known as an *oikonomos,* "steward" or "household manager." Xenophon — best known for his firsthand adventure story the *Anabasis,* about a march inland to the heart of the Persian Empire in a military venture on behalf of Cyrus, a claimant to the throne — wrote a charming little book called *Oikonomikos* to instruct his wife on how to run the household.[1] She was given considerable responsibility.

Such a "science of household management" — more than what we later called "home economics" or "good housekeeping" or "domestic science" — became part of normal Greek philosophizing. Xenophon portrays Socrates as offering instructions on it. Plato and Aristotle included it in their scheme of things.[2] There is an *Oeconomica* attributed to Aristotle (actually a composite of books dated from 300 B.C. to A.D. 400).[3] In the ruins of a villa at Herculaneum, covered with lava by the eruption of Mt. Vesuvius in A.D. 79, was found a treatise on the topic by the philosopher Philodemus.[4] This learned Roman (who actually came from Gadara, in Palestine) wrote of *oikonomia* in the first century B.C. as one of the standard virtues in society.

It must be remembered that the household in antiquity was not only the fundamental unit in social organization but also functioned as an economic entity. In rural areas the "farm family" engaged in agricultural enterprise together. In urban regions, an *oikos* might have been engaged in a common commercial venture (the household of Lydia of Thyatira, in Philippi, in Acts 16:15, comes to mind, with its enterprise in the purple cloth and dyeing business) or even a small manufacturing operation (Priscilla and Aquila, tentmaking or leather goods, Acts 18:3). And it is worth remembering that this social-economic unit of the household might also be bound together by religious ties. For the first few centuries of Christianity, the "house church" was the fundamental unit of ecclesiastical structure.[5]

All this was the setting for the basic meaning of *oikonomia,* the art and science of household management. Etymologically the term meant to administer or manage an *oikos* (from the verb *nemein*, "manage," not the noun *nomos* or "law"). Care of domestic affairs was involved, marked by "husbandry," thrift, frugality, and a host of features summed up under the word "economical." One could even speak of codes or rules for social-economic relationships within a household, called in German *Haustafeln*, "tables of household duties," of the sort reflected in such New Testament passages as Colossians 3:18–4:1; Ephesians 5:21–6:9; and 1 Peter 2:13–3:7, with regard to husband and wife, parents and children, masters and slaves, and the state and the citizen.[6]

2. In the (City-)State

In Greek thought the *oikos*, or household, paralleled the city-state (in Greek, the *polis*).[7] The *polis* was a household writ large, with the same relations and functions as a family but on a larger scale. Hence it was an obvious step to extend the term *oikonomia* to the management of a state, from such relatively small political entities as the city-states of Athens, Corinth, and Sparta to entities as large as the Persian Empire. How one managed such a "household" was the concern in this usage. There was a certain admiration among Greeks for the orderly way in which the Persian king delegated power and ruled in the satrapies through governors and other underlings, including stewards *(oikonomoi)* of all sorts. It is probably from such applications that *oikonomia* sometimes came to have a hierarchical quality to it, connoting levels of administration and management.

This management of a social unit larger than a family appeared sometimes with regard to military affairs — obviously an army had to have a structured organization and a chain of command — but it also came to apply to all sorts of managers and administration in the civil realm. In addition to its use with respect to political life and governmental administration, *oikonomoi* appeared especially with regard to financial affairs, guilds and other societies, and religious cult groups. The number of "stewards" in the service of local authorities, the province, or the empire for keeping records, collecting taxes, or carrying out day-to-day administrative matters was staggering. The title appeared often enough in Greco-Roman cult, for temples and quasi-religious groups, that the phrase Paul uses, "stewards (of the mysteries) of God" (1 Cor. 4:1), would not have sounded strange to Greek ears.[8]

3. Extended to "Arrangement" in General

The next step to note in Greek usage involves an application of *oikonomia* to "arrangement" or arrangements in life generally or in certain specific areas such as literature and rhetoric. Here the sense may either be quite literal or metaphorical. One can speak in medicine of how the human body is "arranged" and of "arranging affairs" in one's life. Much more specific is the application to legal arrangements. The document that served as a last will and testament could be called an *oikonomia*.[9] The word was used in a technical sense in architecture and probably in music.

The most interesting application here for later Christian use may have been the way historians such as Polybius spoke of *oikonomia*. The word could be used in reference to the literary arrangement of their work in the same way it was used in reference to the work of dramatists and other writers of the period, but it also took on the sense at times of an "arrangement" to history that Fortune or the other gods provided and that the historian sought to discover and present to readers. We shall return later to a consideration of ancient views of history and "the economy of God."

An equally striking application occurs in rhetoric, a discipline that was quite the rage among Greeks and Romans both.[10] *Oikonomia* had here to do with how a skilled orator arranged the arguments or related events in his speech so as to make the case as strong as possible. Sometimes this "economic" arrangement differed from straightforward chronological order.

From this last usage it was but a step to usage of *oikonomia* in ethics. There the term could mean how one arranged conduct. It was used specifically in cases in which a person appeared to be doing one thing but intended something else; external actions mask inner purpose. To use a later term, such "economical conduct" was an "accommodation" to circumstances: it suggested one thing while intending another. According to classical Greek and later patristic writers, even God's actions might be interpreted to mean something entirely different from what they purported to show.[11]

This third area of extended meanings is the one least to be seen in the New Testament, if it appears at all. But it would prove immensely influential in the work of later Christian writers.

4. Applied to the World Household

The ultimate extension of *oikonomia*-terminology was to the largest "household" imaginable, that of the world or universe. Behind this extension was a logical progression from *oikos* to *polis* to the *kosmos,* or universe. The world, its various parts, and its peoples were understood to have a certain order to them, an arrangement or regulation by God or nature. This order was not simply provided at the beginning of things but continued providentially in human life and indeed the structure of all things.

The pre-Socratic philosophers spoke of such a scheme of arrangement in nature. They reasoned from this to an "administration" (*oikonomia,* among other words) of the universe. God was viewed as "administrator" managing the affairs of human beings and the whole universe in such a way as to fit the divine design and will.

This fourth area, which involves "the economy of God," provides a background for certain New Testament references and for an expanding application by later Christian writers. It is in fact the most important of the classical-Hellenistic senses for later theology. And it is a sense we would be likely to overlook if we thought of *oikonomia* only as "stewardship."

B. Biblical Usage

1. In the Old Testament

None of this rich Greek background is to be found in the Hebrew Scriptures. There are virtually no Old Testament roots for what the New Testament and Church Fathers did with the *oikonomia* theme. This must be emphasized because some writers have claimed otherwise. Helge Brattgård, for example, has argued that "the content of the biblical idea of stewardship . . . can be traced throughout the entire Bible"; Douglas John Hall states even more strongly that the steward image emerges "only in the Hebraic-Christian sources."[12] Richard Sheef is far more accurate in asserting that "there is no exact equivalent in the Hebrew Old Testament for the English term 'stewardship,' " and he then turns instead to "Basic Theological Presuppositions of the Old Testament" for help.[13] *Oikonomos* occurs only twelve times at most in the Septuagint (a pre-Christian Greek translation of the Hebrew Scriptures), usually to denote a person who is "over the household (*'ăšer ʿal-habbayit)*" of the king or a rich person, and *oikonomia* only twice, both in the passage about Shebna and Eliakim in Isaiah 22 (vv. 19, 21; RSV and NRSV translate the term as "office, authority"). Others have sought to make something of Moses being "entrusted with all [God's] house" (Num. 12:7), but even in the verse's use at Hebrews 3:1-6 the term "steward" is not employed. The official "over the household" was nothing unique to the ancient Israelites; it was common throughout the entire Near East. Indeed, it likely originated under foreign influence on Israel.[14]

So pervasive was the Greek word *oikonomos,* however, that it was brought over as a loanword in Semitic languages; the Greek word was transliterated and written in Hebrew letters.[15]

2. Jesus

Jesus was familiar with such stewards and told a parable about an

16

oikonomos in Luke 16:1-8, whom we call "the dishonest steward" or "the unjust steward."[16] The "faithful steward" theme in 16:10-12 is also reflected in a saying at 12:42 about "the faithful and wise steward, whom his master will set over his household." The entire passage in Luke 12:35-48 can be read on the "Jesus level" as a critique of Jewish leadership in Jesus' day and as an admonition toward "proportionate duty," as Henry J. Cadbury once wrote in connection with 12:48 ("to whom much is given, of him much will be required"). It can be more fully understood on a Lukan level as directed in the Hellenistic church toward leaders of the community and their stewardship of office.[17]

3. The World of Paul

Paul knew about "stewards" too. Galatians 4:2 mentions "guardians and trustees" (*oikonomoi*, or administrators over the property of a minor), and Romans 16:23 quotes greetings from Erastus, a convert who was serving as "treasurer [*oikonomos*] of the city" of Corinth.

The starting point for Paul's own theologizing about the terms is 1 Corinthians 4:1-2, where he speaks of himself, Apollos, and Cephas as "stewards of the mysteries [= openly revealed secrets] of God" — that is, the gospel revelation.[18] In 1 Corinthians 9:17 we get an indication of Paul's deep personal sense of being a steward of God: "I am entrusted with a stewardship" (RSV, "commission"; *oikonomian pepisteumai)* to preach.

The development of the term in later letters makes clear that Paul is the steward and administers the apostolic office; the overall plan is God's, which God manages for our salvation. As Paul puts it in Colossians 1:25, "I am a minister in accord with the *oikonomia of God*" — that is, the role assigned to him by God within the divine economy. It is Ephesians that presents the most breathtaking vision. In Ephesians 3:2 we read of "the stewardship of God's grace that was given to me for you." This task is seen within God's "plan for the fulness of time" (1:10;

17

oikonomia here refers to God's purpose to bring all things into unity). Ephesians 3:9 rounds out the picture by referring to the apostle's assignment to make all persons see "what is the plan [*oikonomia*] of the mystery hidden for ages in God who created all things."

More might be said developing the connections within Paul's thought and on *oikonomia* as the management or administration of the divine plan, which is itself referred to by such terms as "mystery."[19] But for our purposes the references themselves provide sufficient overview.

The New Testament picture can be completed by adding the final three of the eighteen canonical references. There is a characterization of all Christians as "good stewards of God's varied grace" in 1 Peter 4:10. There is a reference to the bishop or overseer as "God's steward" in Titus 1:7. And 1 Timothy 1:4 remains the most perplexing passage, as indicated by the fact that the RSV offers three possible translations. In the preferred rendering of the text, gnostic myths, genealogies, and speculations (cf. 6:20) are contrasted with "the divine training that is in faith" *(oikonomian theou tēn en pistei)*. The first alternate reading is "the divine stewardship which is in faith," and the second speaks of "the divine order" that "belongs to faith," as Moffatt's translation put it. NRSV offers as an alternative to "divine training" only "divine plan," but the exact sense remains open.

4. A Summary

It cannot be claimed that *oikonomia* constitutes a major New Testament theme. It lacks the hundreds of occurrences of a theme such as "covenant" (which is strong in the Old Testament) or "righteousness/justification" (strong in both testaments). It occurs roughly as often as the Greek term we render as "reconciliation" (*katallagē*, [*apo*]*katalassō*, thirteen times). The data base is thus relatively small (though that has not stopped some from maximizing "reconciliation"). But *oikonomia* words in the New

18

Testament do reflect all four main areas of classical use. And they were prominent in the thinking of Christians who came after the New Testament, as can be seen by examining the writings of the later Christian writers.

C. Greek and Latin Writers and the "Economy of God"

The link with this later Christian thinking and application of *oikonomia* was aided by ancient notions of "the economy of God," especially as applied to events in history. We may trace this important linkage by examining several Greek and Latin historians in some detail.

1. Writing Well-Ordered History

About 145 B.C. a Greek statesman named Polybius began to write a *Universal History*. The son of the leader of the famed Achaean League, himself a politician and leader of this union of city-states in southern Greece, Polybius had been carried off to Italy as a hostage when the Romans conquered the region. (Such hostages in Rome helped guarantee the good conduct of the area newly absorbed into Roman control.) In Rome Polybius was befriended by Aemilius Paullus, a former consul from a famous family, a successful general, and a wealthy bibliophile who combined ancient Roman virtues with the Greek love of learning. He ushered Polybius into the cultured circle of the Scipio family. Thus Polybius gained a friendship with Scipio Africanus himself, whom he was able to accompany on the campaign when Rome's long-time enemy Carthage, in North Africa, was finally destroyed in 147 B.C. The next year Polybius was present when Corinth, in his native Greece, was leveled by Roman troops; Corinth became a desolate ruin until reestablished a hundred years later, just a century before Paul preached "Christ crucified" there. Polybius was supplied by his friends with money for research and travel, and he undertook, especially in the last twenty years of his life, to write a history of the rise of Rome to world power, a rise that he had himself witnessed.

In keeping with the rhetorical rules of the day, Polybius paid great attention to the order and arrangement of his *Universal History*. The word he used for this was, in Greek, *oikonomia*, which can also mean "stewardship." There was a reason why Polybius was so concerned with clear arrangement of the material for readers: he assumed that there was an overall arrangement or *oikonomia* to history, a pattern to events provided by divine Fortune (*Tychē*, in Greek). Polybius and like-minded historians paid attention to literary arrangement because there is an arrangement to history itself. "Since Fortune has guided almost all the affairs of the world in one direction," wrote Polybius, referring to Rome's hegemony, or world-rule, "a historian should therefore bring to readers, under one synoptic view, the operations by which Fortune has accomplished her purpose."[20] The theme of Polybius's *Universal History* was thus "the general and comprehensive scheme of events" — in his words, "when and whence the general and comprehensive pattern [*oikonomia*] of events originated." He believed that Rome's development from a village on the Tiber to a superpower represented "the finest and most beneficent of the performances of Fortune" (1.4.1-2)

Eventually, before he died at age 82 (reportedly from injuries received after falling from a horse), Polybius chronicled in forty books the period from 220 to 144 B.C., recounting Rome's expansion into Spain, Africa, and Greece. "Inspired by the rise of Rome, impressed with the strength and stability of her civic . . . institutions, he saw in the protectorate of Rome over Greece . . . an imperial fulfilment which admitted of political analysis."[21] Not without bias, of course, and often with moralizing reflections on events glorifying his patrons, Polybius detailed, Olympiad by Olympiad, the imperial rise of Rome. In the last books of his *Universal History*, as he drew closer to the events nearer his own day, Polybius did grow more critical of Rome, however. The degeneracy of the Senate; the radical, perhaps rabble-rousing attempts at reform by the Gracchi brothers; probably also the sack of Corinth by Roman troops — all these factors shook his faith in Rome's stability, and he began to revise his earlier writings. (It is possible that Polybius was also influenced by Stoic theory about a cyclical degeneration in life to see in his later estimates of the rise of Rome not only Fortune's almost predestined pattern toward Roman preeminence but also a given design in history reflecting evolutionary cycles of rise and decline.)

There were other historians who fell into this same Stoic mold, seeing a divine shape to history. Examples preserved from antiquity include Diodorus of Sicily, who wrote 60-30 B.C., and Dionysius of Halicarnassus, a literary light in Rome during the next two decades, who praised or censured historians for the way they arranged their materials. These writers considered stewardship, or "prudent management of sources," as we may here render the term *oikonomia,* to be incumbent on a historian. Though they do not necessarily stress the arrangement by Fortune of the events they write about, Diodorus does state, in a striking phrase, that authors of universal history are, as it were, "ministers [*hypourgoi*] of some sort, of Divine Providence." He then goes on, in a telling analogy:

> For just as Providence, having brought the orderly arrangement of the visible stars and the natures of men together into one common relationship, continually directs their course through all eternity, apportioning to each that which falls to it by the direction of fate, so likewise the historians, in recording the common affairs of the inhabited world . . . , have made of their treatises a single reckoning of past events and a common clearing-house of knowledge concerning them. (1.1.3-4)[22]

2. Some Conclusions

From such sentiments in Greco-Roman writers prior to the New Testament period, three features stand out with regard to their view of history.

a. They highly valued literary structure in historical accounts. Their word for this was *oikonomia* —management or arrangement of materials, a word also meaning "stewardship." This sense of literary arrangement derives from rhetoric, a much-prized discipline of the day, which dictated that arrangement of content was one of the most important parts of oral presentation and now, for the historian, of written accounts. Dionysius of Halicarnassus considered such arrangement to be the "most artful part" of presenting content, "sought after in all writings."[23] I would add that in recent New Testament studies, attention to influences from Greco-Roman rhetoric on early Christian writings has been prominent and pervasive.[24]

b. Ultimately these historians considered literary arrangement to be an important means for bringing out an overall arrangement in history, a "scheme of events" as Polybius called it, an *oikonomia* in history. On occasion, writers will say that this second factor amounts to a divine pattern in history. Is this "form following function"? Or is it literary form following divine arrangement of events, the *oikonomia* of the things that have occurred? Some may wish to ponder Luke's historical preface to his Gospel, which, as is widely acknowledged, reflects the style of Hellenistic historians:

> Since many have undertaken to set down an orderly account of the events that have been fulfilled among us, just as they were handed on to us by those who from the beginning were eyewitnesses and servants of the word, I too decided, after investigating everything carefully from the very first [*or* for a long time], to write an orderly account for you, most excellent Theophilus, so that you may know the truth concerning the things about which you have been instructed. (1:1-4, NRSV)

The references in Polybius to Tyche, Fortune, or to "the divine" *(to theion)* or "the gods" *(hoi theoi)* ordering history have been hotly debated. Some Polybius scholars dismiss them as conventional references, drawn from Peripatetic philosophy.[25]

Others think Fortune "the one superhuman power in which Polybius had a genuine faith."[26] It has been pointed out that Polybius
was very much a scientific historian, seeking cause and effect
but also, in his own phrase, "the cause of the cause."[27] Is it that
he invokes Fortune only to account for events for which he cannot
find another cause, an explanation for "the irrational" in history?[28] Some two centuries later, Plutarch asked in an essay
whether Rome's greatness was due to virtue (*aretē,* Rome's own
prowess) or fortune granted by the gods.[29] Polybius allowed for
both: such individuals as Scipio exerted powerful influences, but
Fortune also had a role to play. As one modern classicist, W. W.
Fowler, has put it, there exists for Polybius "divine interposition
in the ordinary affairs of the world."[30] And divine Fortune favored
Scipio, just as she humbled the Persians and raised up Macedonia.
But faithless Fortune, says Polybius, "never enters into a treaty
[*asynthetos*] with our life but always defeats our reckoning by
some novel stroke and demonstrates her power by foiling our
expectations" (29.21.5).[31] The irony of it all! How one longs for
a compact (*synthēkē*) or, better yet, a covenant (Hebrew *běrît,*
Greek *diathēkē*) on the basis of which one might consistently
rely on such divine favor and aid!

c. Given this attention to divine arrangement in history and
the writer's literary structure (both expressed by the Greek word
oikonomia, or "stewardship"), it follows that the historian becomes a "steward of history." The actual phrase *oikonomos tēs
historias* never occurs in extant sources, even in Polybius, but
Dionysius came close with his reference to historians as "ministers of Divine Providence."

3. The Underlying "Divine Economy"

If we explore Stoicism further, we find a "theology" or "understanding of God" and a "divine economy" behind all this. It runs
something like this. Just as in a household (Greek *oikos*) there
must be a household manager (the term here is *oikonomos*) —

in Xenophon the manager of the household is the owner's wife; later, a skilled slave was set over the household; the steward in Jesus' parable in Luke 16:1 and 3 is appointed over a larger household or economic unit — so there could be an *oikonomia* or management of a city-state or even an empire. Then, by the greatest extension imaginable, philosophers came to speak of a management of the universe — God's "household management" of the world, if you please. In the orderly arrangement of all things, each person has his or her own place within this administration, under the Master of the house. This Master (*oiko-despotēs*, a term also found in Matt. 13:27; 20:1; 21:33; in parables about God; and, of Jesus, at 10:25) or deity is in Greek Stoicism spoken of also as Fortune, Fate, Nature, or Providence. In God's *oikonomia* of all things, we humans play the role assigned, as stewards. (The term *oikonomos* was used of believers in the New Testament; in Matt. 13:52 a disciple, or "scribe . . . trained for the kingdom of heaven," is likened to "a householder.") But over all, in this type of Greek thought, is one God, the creator deity, the Moral Governor of the universe.[32]

A historian with this outlook might well regard the writer's task to be, as a steward of history, to ferret out any divine pattern to historical events and then to give structure to it in clear literary expression — in short, the divine economy, in an *oikonomia* of language, by an *oikonomos* or steward in history. At least some of this approach and vocabulary was part of the theological *koiné* ("common language") of New Testament times. It was developed by the thinkers, writers, and theologians of the centuries that followed. It is all part of the rich heritage of "stewardship."

Patristic, Medieval, Reformation, and Other Developments in Church History

The startling proliferation of usage for *oikonomia* words and their equivalents in Latin (e.g., *dispensatio*) can be traced in several ways. Edwin Hatch in the Hibbert Lectures a century ago included such material among examples of the influence of Greek ideas and usages on the Christian church.[1] G. L. Prestige, writing in 1936 on God in patristic thought, in studies based on data gathered in England for a great dictionary of the Greek Fathers, included page after page of fascinating examples of how the divine economy was viewed by early Christian writers.[2] The long-promised *Patristic Greek Lexicon,* published in 1961-63, now offers a concise outline of meanings for the terms in Greek writers over the first six to eight centuries.[3] One can proceed chronologically, writer by writer, from Ignatius of Antioch and the other Apostolic Fathers to Irenaeus, Clement of Alexandria, Origen, and such writers as Tertullian and Hippolytus, to say nothing of Eastern theologians in Syriac and other languages. Or one can proceed topically, unfolding the ways in which *oikonomia* came to be applied to the Trinity or to christology. Specialized studies exist in many of these areas. Here we shall proceed first to a general survey of meanings. (Those interested in further illustrations would do well to consult Prestige's book or Lampe's *Lexicon*.) Then we shall put together a picture of how most Christians from the second till the eighteenth century or so thought about the divine economy and sketch some efforts at viewing life and history in its light.

A. Some Uses of *Oikonomia* Words in the Church Fathers: An Overview

1. God's Dispositions and Interpositions

Early Christians of the post–New Testament period inherited from Stoicism and Greek thought generally the idea of a divine economy, the general notion that Zeus (or some other deity) administered a world the gods had made and governed. It is not impossible that the Christians equated this Greek concept with the "kingdom of God" or divine reign that Jesus had preached and the biblical concept of the rule or sovereignty of God. In particular, in light of what they had come to experience in Jesus Christ, these Christians spoke of God's plan to save humankind through the coming, death, and resurrection of Jesus. The New Testament references, especially in Paul, encouraged them to think of an *oikonomia* of God, of which the apostles, church leaders, and all Christians might be a part. All could think of themselves as *oikonomoi*, stewards or administrators of God's saving plan. We can illustrate almost every one of these senses in Christian writers of the second to the sixth centuries.

2. God's Plan and Its Administration

The idea of God managing or administering the universe appears shortly after the completion of the New Testament in the work of the so-called Christian apologists. Writers including Justin Martyr, Tatian, and Athenagoras provide some twenty-two examples of this sort of word usage. The concept became increasingly commonplace as Christians sought to speak meaningfully about the world in which they lived as God's people under the divine governance. Indeed, when historians in the time of Augustine and afterward wanted to explain why Rome had fallen (though God, in their opinion, still ruled the universe), they resorted to some of the same arguments to defend God that Chrysippus and other Stoics had employed against the Epicureans.[4]

3. Jesus' Passion, Resurrection, and Other Events in His Ministry

More important, early Christians applied the idea of the divine economy or stewardship to how God had arranged to accomplish salvation through Jesus Christ. The whole process was God's stewardship or arrangement of events to bring redemption, justification, and life to all who would believe. In particular, the terms were applied to Jesus' passion and resurrection, though other incidents in Jesus' ministry were also referred to as "an economy" or arrangement of grace or as being in accord with God's stewardship of salvation or plan to save. The baptism, the Transfiguration, and the wedding feast at Cana were each referred to as an "arrangement" in the overall scheme.[5]

4. The Incarnation

In particular, Jesus' birth came to be seen as a key step in the whole process. As early as the first decade of the second century, Ignatius of Antioch refers in his epistle to the Ephesians to Jesus' being born of Mary "in accord with the 'arrangement' or economy of God" (18.2). In time, "the economy," with no other adjective or modifier (Greek, *hē oikonomia*) came to mean "the Incarnation" of Christ. This event was viewed as the supreme example of divine arrangement and condescension to save.

5. Old Testament Events

The concept of the economy of God also extended backward, prior to Jesus. Events in the Old Testament were said to have happened "according to the economy of God." For example, the detail at Jonah 4:6 was so described: God "appointed a plant to provide shade" for Jonah at Nineveh (Justin, *Dialogue with Trypho* 107.3).

6. Christology and the Trinity

A further application had to do with use of these terms for the organization, internal disposition, or constitution of Christ or of the Trinity. Applied to Christ, this could refer to his two natures. *Oikonomia* was sometimes used to denote his human nature in contrast to his divinity.

Writers such as Tertullian and Hippolytus applied the term to the Trinity, to the inner organization of the "divine monarchy," or rule by God. Just as the rule of the empire, as a *monarchia* — literally, rule of one person alone — could be divided into several functions, distributed among co-emperors, so also the Godhead, internally, could be presented as an "economic Trinity."[6]

7. Divine Grace and Activity in the Sacraments

Already in the Pauline literature *oikonomia* could mean the administration of God's grace for others (Eph. 3:2). It is not surprising that it later came to mean the dispensation of forgiveness, especially through the sacraments. Among its many applications, *oikonomia* came specifically to refer to the celebration of the Eucharist, "the administration" of the Lord's Supper as we would call it. But the terms could also refer to other "arrangements" to communicate God's grace to men and women.

8. Daily Life and Piety

One of the most important expressions of God's economy came

for believers with regard to daily life. The understanding that God arranges things for our good was by no means confined to the sacred happenings in Israel's history or the coming of Christ. It was not simply the more spectacular events that occurred after Easter in the New Testament, such as Paul's conversion or escape from the earthquake and prison at Philippi, that came to be identified with "an economy" or part of God's stewardship. Things that happened in the daily existence of the simplest believer centuries after Easter were also chalked up to God's interposition into human affairs. Little mercies such as "it became dusk" or "we met a donkey-driver" were ascribed to God's over-all plan and mercy. Prestige reports many examples of this sort of faith in divine Providence.

9. In Ethics and Almsgiving

Inevitably, this concept of the divine economy entered into ethics. It was taught that the disciple should try to imitate God's admin-istration of the world, which would involve good management and thrift. Some called for arrangement of one's life as well; Prestige finds that in some apocryphal literature the word *oikonomia* is used in the sense of "life's work or career or earthly course."[7]

In some cases patristic writings also pick up on the classical Greek usage of *oikonomia* to indicate a stratagem, sharp conni-vance, or even "shady" arrangement.[8] For instance, in a famous passage John Chrysostom explained the quarrel between Peter and Paul at Antioch, described at Galatians 2:11-14, as a sham fight, an "arrangement" to flush out the Judaizers so that the apostles, who had staged the dispute, could together deal with them![9]

A note that all those interested in church finance will appre-ciate is the fact that *oikonomia* also came to mean the adminis-tration of alms, and at times the alms themselves. Church finance, aiding the poor, was viewed as a part of the divine economy.

29

10. In History

It is with regard to history that one of the more important patristic concepts of God's guidance for the world's affairs arose. It involves what C. A. Patrides has called "the grand design."[10] In many ways it dominated thought patterns until the Enlightenment and is still reflected in the work of contemporary writers such as T. S. Eliot. We shall return to this idea later in a more detailed discussion of "the economy of God."

This overview only scratches the surface of the spread of the idea in the second to sixth centuries and beyond, of what *oikonomia,* including stewardship, embraced. One study sees three great Church Fathers as developing three distinct emphases that are nonetheless terminologically related through the vocabulary of *oikonomia* or its Latin equivalents: Irenaeus with "redemptive history" or a series of covenants that God made with humankind, Israel, and the church; Clement of Alexandria through ethical applications; and Tertullian with trinitarian usage.[11]

B. The Economy of God and Subsequent Christian Historiography

The notion of an "economy of God" in the Greco-Roman world seemed ready-made for relating to certain biblical themes. Stoics talked of Zeus's administration of the universe. This *oikonomia* could be related to the kingship or kingdom of God that Jesus had proclaimed. The rule or reign of God also involved a divine plan. The sermons in Acts speak of God's plan (e.g., 2:23; 4:28). In the minds of at least some early Christians, this plan was carried out as the *oikonomia* of God, the divine management or administration of this plan. This meant that the Greek word translated as "stewardship" could be used to refer to God's rule or kingship, the plan of salvation, and the divine administration of that plan. Let us review how Christians in the postapostolic period might have thought about God's *oikonomia* or steward-ship.

1. A Composite Picture of the Divine Oikonomia

Although one might speak of God's stewardship, almost no one referred to God as "steward." This was no doubt because that word had menial connotations. More often God became the ad-ministrator *(ho dioikētēs),* dispenser of goods, or master of the (world) household *(oikodespotēs).* Christ, however, who after all had become a servant (in Greek, *pais,* as at Acts 3:13) or slave *(doulos,* Phil. 2:7) for our salvation, was on occasion called *oikonomos* or steward, though this too is relatively rare.[12] The evidence is such that one is justified, however, in speaking of God's stewardship of the divine plan and the world as part of Christian thought.

God's stewardship was brought into connection with history not by speaking of a divine "stewardship of history" or of Chris-tians as "stewards or makers of history" but rather by seeing God's plan worked out in history, above all through Christ, and then by seeing events in the lives of believers as something God has arranged for them.

Allowing for a variety of ways to translate *oikonomia,* we can put together the following picture from a variety of patristic references.[13]

God's ordering of things, or "providential dispensation," can be seen in creation and then in certain Old Testament and New Testament events. The Lord made special interpositions of grace to provide a plant to shade Jonah (Jon. 4:6), for example, and to call Saul of Tarsus to preach Christ.[14] It was an economy or arrangement by God that led the court official from Ethiopia to meet Philip on the Gaza road.[15] Paul's conversion was a similar act of God, a divine interposition.

Ancient Christians writers explained certain unsavory events in the Old Testament (e.g., a drunken Lot making his own daughters pregnant when they thought the rest of the human race had been wiped out at Sodom [Gen. 19:30-38] or Jacob's several marriages [Gen. 29:15-30]) by characterizing them as "prefigurements" of later salvation through the synagogue and the church.[16] Revelations and prophecies of God's great mysteries — the term now increasingly understood in a Greek sense — provide further examples. Above all, however, such terms were applied to Jesus Christ.

As we have already noted, *oikonomia* was used in reference to the Incarnation from the third century on. It designates that supreme instance of an "arrangement" God has made to save us: the Son came in the flesh *(enanthrōpēsis)*. Already in the early second century, Ignatius of Antioch wrote, "Our God, Jesus the Christ, was carried in the womb of Mary, according to God's plan" or "dispensation of the divine purpose" *(Eph.* 18.2, *kat' oikonomian theou).*[17] This usage was followed and developed by countless Church Fathers and theologians.

But *oikonomia* could also be applied to individual events in the career of Jesus (sense 3 above), whom God the master of the house had sent as part of the divine stewardship or plan or management of salvation. Thus the term might refer, as we have noted, to Jesus' baptism, the Transfiguration, or other incidents in Jesus' ministry, such as the arrangements he made for the entry into Jerusalem or for a room for the Last Supper.[18] These would be the "little *oikonomiai,*" or arrangements or interpositions of grace within the big *oikonomia,* the Incarnation or God's supreme arrangement to deliver women and men. The terminology was employed especially in references to Christ's passion and resurrection — for example, "the savior completed on his cross the divine *oikonomia*"; Irenaeus refers to the *oikonomia* when Christ was nailed to the tree.[19]

From such references it is but a step to employ *oikonomia* in christological discussions (sense 6 above) in reference to the person of Christ, human and divine, in reference to his human nature alone, or in reference to the way the divine lord accommodated himself to conditions of human existence. At times the term was used to refer to the "arrangement" within the Godhead that we call the Trinity — in particular, the distribution of functions between the Father and the Son. There developed, as we have already noted, one relatively early explanation of the triune God in terms of an "economic Trinity." In describing the "interior organization" of the divine unity, Tertullian employed "monarchy" for the single dominion of the One God but "economy" (Latin, *dispensatio*) for the "arrangement" of functions and persons of the Trinity.

But God's dispensations, interpositions, and arrangements did not cease with Christ. G. L. Prestige records a host of examples showing how people saw God continuing to arrange things mercifully in their lives (sense 8, above). Monks in the desert had a vivid sense of small mercies from God's hand. "God did us this economy that neither did we freeze in winter nor does the heat injure us in summer," said one.[20] In another instance the death of an old man is said to have taken place "by the economy of God."[21] The historian Eusebius asserts that the providence of heaven put it into the mind of the Emperor Tiberius by an economy not to persecute Christians.[22] We may quote Prestige and agree with him: "Enough has been said to indicate the extent to which the Greek Fathers recognized, in principle and in detail, the providential activity of God in nature, human history, and the sphere of grace."[23]

It is revealing that the patristic writers used *oikonomia* in reference to the operation of divine grace in the sacraments (sense 7, above) much as we do in the phrase "the administration of Holy Communion." Epiphanius used the term "the Economy" as a synonym for the eucharistic service, but it was also used to refer to remission of sins and the washing of regeneration.[24] To the best of my knowledge, it is not employed by these writers to refer to the human response, to our stewardship, with regard to sacraments or history. One might be an *oikonomos,* or dispenser of alms or of penance, but hardly of history. As one interpreter of Ignatius puts it, "the divine plan" (*Eph.* 20.1) has to do "(subjectively) with faith and love" on our part toward God but "objectively with Christ's passion or resurrection" for us.[25] A pastor, according to Gregory of Nazianzus, was an *oikonomos* of souls and dispenser of the word.[26] In such ways the *oikonomia* of God worked, but the stewardship was, in the final analysis, really *God's*.

2. The Beginnings of Christian Historiography

The understanding of economy outlined above was interconnected over the centuries with views of history in various Christian writers. Eusebius, Bishop of Caesarea, sometimes called "the father of Church History," wrote an ecclesiastical history about the first three centuries of Christianity, a life of Constantine, and treatises on God's preparation for and demonstration of the gospel.[27] R. L. P. Milburn rightly terms his *Historia Ekklēsiastikē* "straightforward chronicle," but his chronology set patterns imitated for centuries.[28] Throughout his works, Eusebius views God as the one who dispenses all things, in nature and history. He variously recounts events during persecution as a great economy of God[29] and cites a Christian of Alexandria testifying to "the wondrous dispensation of God toward us."[30] He saw the acceptance of Christianity by Constantine and, in turn, the declaration of Christianity as state religion as the high point in all history, what Patrides describes as "the terminal point in God's promises to mankind." On the other hand, Eusebius muted and "neglected the ultimate end" (eschatology) "and thereby limited drastically his vision of history."[31] We may call Eusebius's work a chronological history with divine *oikonomiai* studding its course, which Providence was guiding.

Nowadays people speak rather glibly and usually disparagingly of a "Constantinian age." Douglas John Hall, in particular, characterizes the state establishment of Christianity as a terrible mistake (just the reverse of Eusebius's opinion), charging that it led to an "imperial church" in which "stewardship" suffered immensely.[32] But the facts of history have to be considered more carefully. We can scarcely justify a picture of a smooth-running Roman bureaucracy dominating the world and stifling Christian witness. In actuality the end of persecution by the state allowed Christians breathing space to develop their way of life, and state support allowed for many material gains, including production of such biblical manuscripts as Sinaiticus (‭א‬) and Vaticanus (B). But not long after Constantine adopted Christianity, the Empire was racked by division, and barbarian hordes overran much of it. In the fifth century Rome itself was sacked three times, first by the Goths, then the Huns, and last of all by the Vandals. The traditional date for the "fall" of Rome is A.D. 476. Pagan intellectuals charged that all the misfortunes of the day were due to the Empire's having become Christian. Hence ecclesiastical historians had a new task.

Augustine was interested in this matter and encouraged Paulus Orosius, a Spaniard, to write his *History in Answer to the Pagans*.[33] Part of his answer was to survey all the catastrophes that had befallen the world in pagan times; these could not be blamed on Christianity, and they were far worse than recent vicissitudes. Convinced that "one God has directed the course of history,"[34] he also disentangled Christianity from the dying Empire and thus pointed the way to the church as the social institution in which, indeed, civilization would survive in subsequent centuries, especially in the West. Orosius's views on many matters stood until the seventeenth century. Yet his attempts to schematize history into an orderly pattern of four world empires (Assyria, Rome, Macedon, Carthage) led him to manipulate datings.[35]

A similar chronographer-historian was Sulpicius Severus, in France. He summarized world history from the creation to A.D. 400, in Latin,[36] with such style and good critical judgment that Edward Gibbon, who condemned Orosius's work as "pious nonsense," later "hailed Sulpicius as 'a correct and original writer.' "[37]

More poignant are the words of Salvian of Marseilles, who, faced with invasion of his land by the Franks and the deterioration of Roman life, asked "why, if everything in the world is controlled by the . . . governance . . . of God . . . , why . . . the fortune of good men is harder than that of the wicked."[38] We humans do not know the ultimate answer, but Salvian advanced two arguments for dealing with the problem. First, these oddities of world history "do not occur because of the negligence or inattention of God but are permitted by his wise ordinance."[39] That is an argument used earlier by Stoics to defend the economy of God against the Epicureans. Second, these disasters are deserved. Faults of character lead to punishment. The wickedness of the Roman Empire brings God's wrath. That smacks more of the biblical prophet than the Stoic philosopher. A God of justice rules history, "a most just judge."[40]

Dionysius Exiguus, a Scythian monk who labored in Rome, deserves mention because of how he reshaped chronology in a way that reflects the divine economy to this very day. Earlier historians had dated events by the reigns of Roman rulers, most recently in Dionysius's day from the accession of Diocletian in A.D. 284. Such a system became unwieldy, however, as Roman emperors became a thing of the past, with the Empire's decay and dissolution. And why should a Christian date things from the accession of Diocletian, persecutor of the church that he was? So Dionysius, when assigned the task of creating a new Easter cycle, abandoned the old scheme and accepted 753 A.U.C. (for the Latin *ab urbe condida*) as the date for the birth of Christ. That is, Jesus' birth in Bethlehem was fixed at a point in time by reckoning "from the founding of the city" of Rome. The year Dionysius reckoned to begin nine months before that birth, on March 25, the date of the Annunciation by an angel to Mary that she would bear a child, Jesus. Events were then recorded as A.D., *anno domini,* or "in the year of our Lord," and, as we put it in

English, "B.C.," before Christ (in Latin, A.C., *ante Christum*). Dionysius never realized how widespread his somewhat erroneous system would become, for it was a hundred years after his death that it was adopted in England and Spain and not by the Vatican till (A.D.) 963.[41] Ever since, this confessional statement about Christ — namely, that Jesus splits the eras of time and history in half — has been adopted almost universally. The economy of God, in the sense of Christ's Incarnation, dominates the measuring of time for Christians and most others.

Among the more significant Christian figures to write on historical matters were Irenaeus and Augustine. Irenaeus, of Lyons (ca. 130-200), turned to history in his efforts to refute the theories of the Gnostic speculative thinkers of his day. His great emphasis was on the Incarnation of Christ, whose full humanity provides the clue for what human beings should be. Irenaeus's overview of history is covenantal. In some places he speaks in terms of two covenants, related to the Old and New Testaments; elsewhere he speaks in terms of four covenants — with Adam, Noah, Moses, and Christ (sometimes Abraham replaces Adam in the text). Irenaeus is the forerunner of most later schemes of "salvation history" *(Heilsgeschichte)*.

Augustine, working against the backdrop of the fall of Rome to Alaric in 410 and the threatened extinction of Christian civilization before the onslaughts of wild tribal hordes, undertook to compose a Christian philosophy of history. The result was *The City of God against the Pagans,* written in twenty-two books between the years 413 and 426.[42] It is not Rome that is "the eternal city," he argued, but a "city of God" beyond, in the kingdom of God. This city is to be contrasted with an earthly city which is the city of the devil. The latter is marked by self-love, the former by love of God. The climax of this conflicting history will be the last judgment. From the divine vantage point, all history can be viewed *sub specie aeternitatis,* "under the aspect of eternity." Within this overall schema Augustine posited six ages: (1) from Adam to Noah, (2) from Noah to Abraham,

(3) from Abraham to David, (4) from David to the Babylonian captivity, (5) from the exile to the Incarnation, and (6) from Christ's birth till the parousia. (The three divisions in Israel's history mentioned in Matthew 1:17 provide a biblical starting point for such an outline; Augustine is more detailed.) Still to come was a Seventh Age, which would round out the sequence. In all this the church relates to the kingdom of God and is where God's "city" takes shape.

3. The Middle Ages, the Reformation, and Beyond

In the centuries from Augustine to the Reformation, as the Constantinian Empire split and then disappeared first in the West and later in the East, one can, of course, trace out how the church took over hegemony at many points. This church was no longer an imperial establishment, but it reflected the rise of something in the place of an empire governed by Caesar from Rome. The institution of the church in the West was increasingly directed by the pope. The Eastern church developed in its own way, under Byzantium and in other great sees. It was a period in which Christian leaders literally made history. Protestants may not agree on papal claims as they developed, and Roman Catholics since Vatican II may think differently about such ecclesiastical triumphalism, but here, surely, was a church triumphant.

There were a number of "world histories" written in the medieval period that reflect the resulting outlook, though with interesting modifications. Otto, Bishop of Freising in the twelfth century, who fought on a crusade and introduced the study of Aristotle into Germany, composed a *Chronicon,* or "History of the Two Cities." He argued that Augustine's two cities had become united in the Catholic Church. His work is marked by a streak of pessimism, however, stemming from his conviction that the last days were approaching. Intimations of judgment and eschatology mark his historical account of his own day. Here was history, from alpha to omega, written from the omega point. In the thirteenth century the English Benedictine Matthew Paris wrote a *Chronica Majora,* covering events from the creation to 1259. As he approaches his own day, Paris grows increasingly critical of ecclesiastical abuses, particularly on the part of certain popes.[43] With variations of one sort or another, all these writers were, however, presenting what they saw as the "grand design of God" expressed in human history.[44]

Hall speaks of a "thin tradition," or "the disinherited," as a sort of underground movement preserving the "stewardship" idea throughout the so-called Constantinian period (which, by his reckoning, runs from 312 till the mid-twentieth century).[45] Others have preferred to speak of a "grand design" to history that Christians contemplated throughout many of these centuries, an argument that they developed often quite apart from the state, indeed at times within a church at odds with secular rulers of various countries (papal domination in contrast to "caesaropapism"). I would agree that a kind of underground movement did maintain an alternate vision during this period, but I would characterize it as an *apocalyptic* underground, a tradition inspired by the symbols of apocalyptic writings in the Bible and the dreams of those outside the social and power structures. In his study of groups that held to this sort of vision, Norman Cohn underscores the eschatological, apocalyptic impulse that has historically motivated them and continues to do so today.[46]

An apocalyptic approach was presented around the year 1200 in several writings by Joachim of Fiore, a Cistercian monk of great piety and learning, who established his own monastery in Calabria, in southern Italy.[47] His trinitarian view of history was destined to have great influence. In some ways, though people may not realize it, his analysis has continued to appear to our own day in all dispensational schemes for looking at history. Joachim reworked the idea that history could be understood in terms of eras of nature, law, and grace, assigning each of the three eras more specifically to God the Father, God the Son, and God the Holy Spirit, respectively. He collapsed the eras of nature

39

and law into one and associated it with the time between Adam and Christ, referring to it as the *ordo conjugatorum,* or age of the married. Then, with the coming of Christ, he taught, humanity entered the period of the Son, an era encompassing the time from the Incarnation to Joachim's own day. He described this era as the *ordo clericorum,* or age of the clergy. He then argued that commencing with his writings, a new era was dawning — the age of the Holy Spirit, *ordo monachorum* or *contemplantium.* This time of monks and contemplatives was to be an age of the Spirit, of people living in the liberty that proceeds from the Old and New Testaments.

Joachim's writings included a Book of Concord (a harmony of the Old and New Testaments) and a commentary on the book of Revelation. His followers put together an anthology on "the eternal gospel," *Evangelium aeternum,* which was far more controversial and was condemned by the church.[48] "Joachimism," a movement associated with these various writings, spread in the thirteenth and following centuries, in a variety of forms. Adherents propounded the dispensationalist theme of a new age about to dawn, an age that would go beyond the "new creation" that had begun with the coming of Jesus Christ. It spawned both refined, learned analyses of the topic and monastic and lay movements, sometimes raucous ones, that advocated all sorts of radical ideas. Its concept of a *Medium Aevum,* between the age of the Father and that of the Spirit, gave us the term "Middle Ages" to identify the period roughly from 500 to 1500. Its alluring vision of a better hope about to come to fruition attracted all sorts of groups, right down to Hitler's "Third Reich," which was supposed to last a thousand years.

When the Reformation movement began, there were thus a variety of options for viewing history. Different strands of the Protestant movement took up different lines of thought. The dominant ecclesiastical view equated the Church of Rome with the kingdom of God; Rome was characterized in a new sense as the eternal city, and it was taught that to break with the Roman hierarchy and Christ's vicar, the pope, was to forfeit connection with Christ himself. The radical, apocalyptic view held that the kingdom of God had freshly and directly come into human history. This sort of approach is evident in the thought of Thomas Münzer and in the claim that the kingdom would arrive on Easter day in 1530 in the German city of Münster.

Luther rejected both the Roman Catholic and apocalyptic options and argued instead that God governs in two ways, through the divine law and justice on the one hand and through love on the other. The first mode applies to all people, whether they acknowledge it or not; it is a secret rule, unavowed by many but nonetheless real. The second method holds sway in the church when Christ is confessed and people openly acknowledge God's kingdom in their lives.[49] Following another line of development, Calvin put far greater emphasis on God's sovereignty, and in the "experiment at Geneva" he tried to construct an actual Christian city-state.

The breakdown of the "grand design" may have been anticipated in some of the events of the late Middle Ages and the strain of the Reformation, but it arrived with certainty in the growth of rationalism and the coming of the Enlightenment. As rationalists developed methods for interrogating and testing documents from the past, they also began to champion critical history as a goal. Many began to ask whether things really were as the church maintained — in the "Donation of Constantine," for example. This document reported how the Emperor had conferred on Pope Sylvester I (who reigned 314-35) primacy over all sorts of ecclesiastical centers and many states and cities of western Europe. It helped solidify and extend papal power. But research by Lorenzo Valla and others demonstrated the document to be a Frankish forgery of the eighth or ninth century. In time, this sort of critical methodology was applied to the Bible itself, with regard to the creation story, miracles, and other aspects of its content. Thus the acids of modernity began to erode the design to history that had dominated for so many centuries.[50]

This inquiring spirit, coupled with events of the day and new currents of thought, challenged the notion even of Providence, which had held sway from pre-Christian times and apart from the Bible. The great Lisbon earthquake of 1755 raised questions about the reign of a loving God in nature. In *Candide* Voltaire ridiculed the notion that we live in "the best of all possible worlds."[51] More recently the Holocaust made Jews and at least some Christians question whether belief in Providence or even in God is still possible. The sixties brought the rise of the "God is dead" movement. The "economy of God" with its "grand design" had come face to face with modernity.

We are thus left with questions about history, God, the divine economy, and stewardship. Is all sheer chaos, meaningless to faith? Or is there a pattern to it, some kind of "salvation history"? Can Christians say anything about history between the traditional idea of a "grand pattern" and the assertion that history is nothing more than "a tale told by an idiot, full of sound and fury, signifying nothing"?

Recent Views on the Divine Economy in History and Stewardship

"Stewardship" as a theme in church life came into existence, especially in North America, as the older idea of "the economy of God" and a grand design to history was going into eclipse. Being a good steward, particularly of money, developed as a way of life not, however, knowingly and consciously *because* the old order had disappeared but *assuming* and *in light of it.* Much of the biblical story, into which we all fit as stewards of the grace of God in the gospel's missionary advance, was still heard and heeded, and the notion of a plan of God, indeed of rewards from God, sparked early efforts at stewardship in the United States.

It will therefore be helpful to take note of some Christian views of history in the nineteenth and twentieth centuries that attempted to preserve the idea of the "grand design" of God. Then we will turn to the rise of the stewardship movement. Some scholars (e.g., Douglas John Hall) have seen a link between these two trends of history and stewardship. New Testament scholar Oscar Cullmann has employed the Greek word *oikonomia* in his view of history and salvation. And the Second Vatican Council can be said to have picked up on the notions of divine economy and Christian responsibility in the world, though without specifically using the chiefly Protestant word "stewardship."

STEWARDSHIP AND THE ECONOMY OF GOD

A. History and Theology in Recent Times

Over the centuries, as we have seen, the Church Fathers and the Reformers discerned certain patterns in history. Scholars in the past two centuries have discerned a variety of different patterns, including those in the *Heilsgeschichte* ("salvation history") school, in liberal Protestantism, in such Catholic philosophers as Christopher Dawson and Martin D'Arcy, and in Protestant theologians like Reinhold Niebuhr and Paul Tillich.[1]

It has been during this more recent period that historical studies have came of age. Nothing short of a revolution was effected in nineteenth-century Germany by Leopold von Ranke and others in their quest for objective precision about what really happened in history, "wie es eigentlich gewesen." There came also the reaction in R. G. Collingwood and others that subjectivity is required: how can one piece together the past without having been excited by one's own participation in history and existence?[2] Subsequently there have been various types of "revisionist" history and the "new history," the French Annales School, which swarms over all sorts of available data to try to create a history not of kings and battles but of ordinary people in everyday settings; the somewhat related "cliometricians" with their statistics; and feminist history, black history, liberation theology, and people and ideologies of all sorts wearing historians' robes.

There have also been attempts to speak on history among the churches. Notable attempts in this vein include the Second Vatican Council's document *Gaudium et Spes* (the "Pastoral Constitution on the Church in the Modern World," 1965), and the Faith and Order Statement of the World Council of Churches "God in Nature and History" (1967).[3] The former document surveys a changing world from the perspective of Christ as the Alpha and Omega, the center of the human race and goal of human history (#45). The latter speaks of "the God who acts" — to use a phrase common in work of such biblical scholars as

G. Ernest Wright and Floyd V. Filson[4] — and seeks to relate this God of the Bible who acts in history to the world of nature. This emphasis in the 1967 Faith and Order statement reflected a direction set within the World Council of Churches by the address of Joseph A. Sittler, Jr., to the New Delhi Assembly in 1961, in which he attempted to outflank impasses in ecclesiology by appealing to the whole world of creation as the arena for God's work or stewardship.[5]

We may note a few key, often contrasting, voices in this pluralistic age of ours, to show the variety of views Christian believers have adopted concerning history.

1. Latourette and Butterfield

Some voices have winsomely continued to express traditional Christian views. It has been claimed that by the time of World War II the title "Christian historian" had become an anachronism if not a contradiction in terms. But Kenneth Scott Latourette of Yale helped revive publicly the notion that faith is an acceptable presupposition to one's work as a historian.[6] Latourette combined history with the mission expansion of Christianity. A more significant voice, however, is probably that of Herbert Butterfield, Regius Professor of Modern History at Cambridge and Methodist lay preacher.

A series of lectures that Butterfield delivered in 1948, subsequently published under the title *Christianity and History,* has been hailed as "perhaps the single most distinguished statement by a twentieth-century Christian historian."[7] In many ways Butterfield had earlier been simply a technical historian, writing on such topics as Napoleon or the Whig interpretation of history until 1944 or so, when his Christian concerns became overt. Events of the Second World War, it can be argued, were a factor in changing his focus. In any event, it is striking to note his insistence in *Christianity and History* on the role of sin in the human predicament. There are also indications that he considered

45

the defeat of Germany in World War II as divine judgment on "Hohenzollernism."[8]

It is more important for our purposes, however, to note the extent to which Butterfield's stance conforms to the old idea of a "stewardship of history" such as was outlined for Polybius, and how Butterfield differs at points.

a. Butterfield strongly defended the role of *providence in the historical order* (*CH,* pp. 93-112). He was personally convinced that Providence had led him in his own career, including the decision to present the 1948 lecture series. He asserts that divine Providence lies "in the very constitution of things" (*CH,* p. 95). "I am unable to see how a man can find the hand of God in secular history, unless he has first found that he has had an assurance of it in personal experience" (*CH,* p. 107). On whether people believe in God or not "depends their whole interpretation of history" (*CH,* p. 113). As for himself, Butterfield wrote in his diary that on 4 February 1926 he had seen God in Cambridge on Trumpington Road.[9]

b. He maintained that it is emphatically part of the historian's task to engage in *political and social analysis.* Certainly he did so in many of his own books and essays.

c. He prized *literary structure* and expression highly. Butterfield's early works show a romantic, literary side, and he leaned toward Trevelyan's view of history as an art rather than J. B. Bury's insistence that it is a science.[10]

d. While carrying out his analyses of history from a certain vantage point of Providence, Butterfield nonetheless eschewed *moral judgments.* He contended that historians should especially avoid "wars of righteousness," since there is a grave risk that they might be misled in their judgments by presumptions of their own righteousness (*CH,* pp. 138-40). This is likely a reflection of his acute awareness of sin. The influence of the fall looms large in his work (see, e.g., *CH,* p. 106). "It is essential," he wrote, "*not* to have faith in human nature" (*CH,* p. 47; italics mine). Hence also his closing advice: "Hold to Christ, and for the rest be totally uncommitted" (*CH,* p. 146).

e. Butterfield makes a famous analogy to an orchestra that is pertinent with respect to *history-making*. Human beings are like musicians, free to play what we wish, but God the composer works to create harmony and pull the notes together. Humans may make history in the short run, but God brings about the long-range results (*CH,* pp. 94-95). The history-making goes on over our heads (*CH,* p. 96). We use spirals, cycles, diagrams of forces colliding, patterns, and symbols to describe such history-making when "History herself" takes "a hand in the game," when it is "as though an intelligence were moving over the sky, taking its bearings afresh after everything men do, and making its decisions as it goes along" (*CH,* pp. 108-9) — like that celestial symphony conductor again. In fact, Butterfield seems to come close to the ancient patristic understanding when he speaks of "providential dispositions" or "workings of history" in which "must be felt the movement of a living God" (*CH,* p. 111). But with regard to these workings, he is speaking more with respect to the inner moral world of the individual than to a culmination of all history (*CH,* pp. 111-12). This helps to explain his advice to trust Providence, to float on it as an agency living in ourselves and running through all history, especially the "special Providence" with which Christians can be in alliance (*CH,* p. 112).

But one must ask if Butterfield's revival of the doctrine of Providence in his writings, lacking as it does any real christology, eschatology, or ecclesiology, is specifically Christian enough. William A. Speck has questioned whether Butterfield's advocacy of a suspension of moral judgments is supportable in the face of something like the Vietnam conflict or genocide.[11]

2. Crisis Theology: Barth, Bultmann, Brunner, and Löwith

Another voice to heed among the theological currents that began in reaction to the liberalism that dominated so much of the nineteenth and early twentieth centuries is that of neo-orthodoxy, or "crisis theology." Especially pertinent is Karl Löwith, even though he is less well known than Karl Barth, Rudolf Bultmann, or Emil Brunner. Löwith once wrote that Butterfield was "a wise historian and a Christian" but insisted that that was different from saying he was a "Christian historian."[12] The latter phrase is, from the neo-orthodox standpoint, a contradiction in terms. How so?

Protestant liberalism, as exemplified in Albrecht Ritschl's theology, had viewed the kingdom which Jesus taught as coming about through the social, moral, and political forces of history.[13] Humanity was evolving into the divine Commonwealth. But Ritschl's own son-in-law, Johannes Weiss, and then Albert Schweitzer showed how Jesus' proclamation was far more apocalyptic in tone and looked to the end of all human history by divine catastrophic intervention.[14] Moreover, two world wars and the worldwide economic depression shattered, at least in Europe, all hopes of evolutionary progress. In Thomas Hardy's gloomy couplet,

> After two thousand years of saying mass,
> We've got as far as poison gas.

Or, in a more modern paraphrase,

> After twenty centuries of Christian mission,
> We've arrived at nuclear fission.

Barth sundered all pretense about progress or about the Christian community leading general history to fulfillment. History, he argued, is at best a backdrop to the call and sustenance of the covenant community. We need not sketch out here all that crisis theologians said about the Word of God striking perpendicularly from above to call individuals to decision and salvation in Christ; our interest is in their view of history. Their perspective stands in stark contrast to that of the patristic writers. They paint history as a directionless sequence, cut off from the redemptive activity of God's Word. They insist that true life is available to persons only through the proclamation of the gospel, not the historical process.

As Langdon Gilkey put it, "History is the realm of meaningless-ness, sin, and death . . . totally divorced from the immanent principle of salvation."[15] Löwith goes so far as to suggest that the proper Christian approach to history ought to be to reject it. He argues that New Testament presents history as a realm of chaos ruled by Satan; it is what the biblical writers call "this age," in contrast to God's "age to come."[16] To suppose that there can be a specifically "Christian" approach to "this age" is "nonsense."[17] Who wants or needs it? It is certainly not in the plan of God! The Bible's eschatological vision has, according to the neo-orthodox understanding, all too often been transformed into secular visions of progress, via Augustine and Hegel and Marx.[18]

Bultmann hewed to this line in his 1955 Gifford lectures in Edinburgh, published as *History and Eschatology*. Blending radical biblical criticism with existentialism, he insisted that human history as history is meaningless. *"The meaning in history lies always in the present";* "do not look around yourself into universal history, you must look into your own personal history."[19] The paradox of Christian existence is that we live as historical beings in this world and at the same time experience each instant as eschatological — a phrase, by the way, that is also found in Butterfield's *Christianity and History* (p. 121).

Later in his *Church Dogmatics* (III/3/XI), Karl Barth modified his initial anti-historicism and accommodated a doctrine of Providence, and Niebuhr and Tillich also wrestled more fully with the meaning of history. Generally, however, such neo-orthodox theologians as Nicolas Berdyaev and Brunner were negative about the concept of God in history. For his part, Löwith drew on the distinction between the two German terms for "history" — *Historie* and *Geschichte*.[20] He saw *Historie* as theologically meaningless, and *Geschichte* as the interpretation by faith of the meaning of Jesus Christ as grace, grace for a reconciliation with God that lies outside general history, in our personal experience. Saving faith is a matter of personal experience, not historical development. "In Christianity the history of salvation is related to the salvation of each single soul, regardless of racial, social, and political status," said Löwith, "and the contribution of the nations to the Kingdom of God is measured by the number of the elect, not by any corporate achievement or failure."[21]

Finally, we may note a point about the neo-orthodox understanding of "making history." Gilkey contrasts neo-orthodoxy with Calvinism on the one hand, with its stress on the sovereignty of God, the God who elects, and with liberal Christianity on the other hand, with its vision of Christians contributing to the kingdom in history by their daily actions. He argues that neo-orthodoxy grants a certain autonomy to human beings, a capacity to respond to divine grace. In this sense, there is a human "freedom to be self-creative and so to be creative as 'maker' of history."[22] The events of history can therefore be said to stem from human, not divine, decisions. But this turns out to be a dreadful freedom, typically botched, for God is not at work in this history but only in the world of personal existence where the Word meets the response of faith. Reactions to these implications of neo-orthodoxy later arose in the Pannenberg school, new eschatological emphases, and "political theology."

3. Douglas John Hall and Stewardship

The third and final voice that must be emphasized is that of a professor of systematic theology at McGill University in Montreal, Douglas John Hall. Three of his books — *The Steward* (1982), *Christian Mission* (1985), and *Imaging God* (1986) — grew out of an extended engagement with the stewardship movement in North America under the aegis of the Commission for Stewardship of the National Council of the Churches of Christ in the U.S.A. Out of the considerable riches of these works, in which Hall broadens the concept of "stewardship" to encompass even mission as "the whole posture called Christian" in a "stewardship of all believers," we shall take special note of his theological stance toward history.

Hall's sympathies plainly lie with Protestant liberalism,[23] but he has also been influenced by Niebuhr, John Bennett (of Union Theological Seminary, New York), and Luther's theology of the cross.[24] Despite his use of indigenous North American concepts of stewardship and political theologies of liberation, Hall nonetheless maintains a love-hate relationship with European (especially German) theology. The following points leap out regarding his treatment of history:

a. History itself is not prominent in Hall's discussion, in spite of his emphasis on not abandoning this world.[25] This is in part because his interest in the world is focused principally on developing a "theology of nature"[26] and perhaps also because he characterizes the whole "Constantinian period" (by which he means the period stretching from the time of Constantine in the fourth century until quite recent history) as an era of "imperial bondage."

b. He does, however, strike some new notes with regard to the liberal view of history.

(1) He contends that we must be "alert to the negative dimension of historical experience"[27] — a note no doubt inherited from neo-orthodoxy.

(2) Acknowledging with approval the disestablishment of the formerly dominant mainline Protestant denominations, Hall argues that "smaller is better." He invokes the theology of the cross to suggest that success in evangelism is actually a betrayal of the gospel: authentic mission is not a matter of being "enormously successful" but of caring for the earth with others.[28]

(3) Does the wish to identify with the "thin tradition" of the "disinherited" and "minorities" through the centuries not put Hall closer to the apocalyptic mind-set than he may wish to be?[29]

In an overly searing critique presented in a series of lectures to pastors of the United Church of Christ, Luke T. Johnson characterized Hall's approach as "simplistic on history."[30] I believe it would be more accurate to say that the stewardship of history was not in Hall's immediate perspective as he wrote. What he has done is to move stewardship into new areas, especially ecological concerns — a far cry from what it often had been in the churches.

B. A History of Stewardship in the Churches and Beyond

Although *oikonomia* had long been associated with a divine plan or economy of God in history and nature, the other major sense of the word — the sense that the King James Version of 1611 gives it in Luke 16, the Pauline writings, and elsewhere, from the Anglo-Saxon *sty-ward* — experienced a new development in what became, broadly speaking, "the stewardship movement." Anglican, Eastern Orthodox, and other theologies might go on speaking of "God's oeconomy" (to use the old-fashioned spelling), but Protestant theology carried the "steward" manifestation to new heights of emphasis in church life.

This thing called stewardship is very much a North American contribution to church practice and thought. Indeed, as Helge Brattgård points out in his book on the topic, one indication of this situation is the fact that many languages have no word for stewardship. In German, for example, the Luther Bible employs *Haushalterschaft* and, for "steward," *Haushalter* at Luke 16 and elsewhere. Unfortunately, in German those words have a menial, servile connotation (as indeed the Greek did at times). Accordingly there have been attempts in German Protestant circles to substitute *Treuhändlerschaft,* denoting the ability to be a faithful handler of God's gifts, or even to create a word drawing on the English term, *die Stewardschiffe.*[31] (Some may think it poetic justice that German has no word for this concept, since English-speaking theologians have borrowed so many technical terms from the German, but it points to how English or really American this concept is.) Along with one other term from English for a major theological doctrine — "atonement" — stewardship is clearly a North American contribution to the church universal.

All this does not mean that no one besides Canadian and U.S. church leaders have dealt with the topic. Witness the book by Brattgård, who became a bishop in the Church of Sweden, or, much earlier, *Christian Giving,* by V. S. Azariah, Bishop of Dornakal, India.[32]

Something of the history of our topic will make the "Made in U.S.A." nature of stewardship more clear. *The Story of Stewardship in the United States of America,* by George A. E. Salstrand, provides a convenient overview.[33] Despite the implications of the title, I would venture to say that the story did not differ profoundly in Canada or the British Isles.

1. Ministerial Support, Missions, and Stewardship till the Great Awakening

Salstrand traces the concerns that led to the stewardship movement back to colonial times and the need for financial support for ministers. How could churches provide for clergy in an unsettled environment, and especially in missionary situations, when there was no state support? The problem grew larger with the rise of modern missions overseas. How could workers be supported in that undertaking?[34]

As early as 1832 the minister of First Church (Congregational) in New Haven, Connecticut, Leonard Bacon, was preaching a sermon entitled "The Christian Doctrine of Stewardship." The text was Acts 9:6, "Lord, what wilt thou have me to do?" Bacon's answer focused on "the right use of property on Christian principles." In 1836 Pharcellus Church, a Baptist of Rochester, New York, wrote a volume entitled *The Philosophy of Benevolence.* And the evangelist Charles Finney set forth "seven accountabilities of men as God's stewards," among them being use of time, talents, and possessions and the cultivation of concern for the souls of others.[35]

In the 1840s and '50s there took place what Salstrand calls "the great stewardship awakening." Horace Bushnell called for one more revival, this time a revival of Christian stewardship, or the "consecration of the money power of the church of God." Echoing John Wesley, others argued that it was the duty of some men to make a great deal of money and to be wholly consecrated with it to the expansion of the kingdom. A formal statement appeared in 1858 from the Old School Presbyterians, the first such denominational address to the topic: "Every man is a steward of God in the use and management of talents, time, and substance which God has entrusted to him"; the "grace of charity" could be strengthened by exercise on the part of most believers.[36]

2. The Rediscovery of the Tithe

If there was a decline in stewardship after the Civil War, the next impetus was "the rediscovery of the tithe," according to Salstrand.[37] A Chicago businessman named Thomas Kane was the pioneer here. In 1876 he said he knew of no one other than himself who was a tither. By 1890 he had personally published millions of pamphlets on the subject and founded "The Layman Foundation," which continued the work of this pioneer "layman," as he called himself. St. Stephen's Episcopal Church in the Manayunk section of Philadelphia turned to tithing in 1877. Wesley Chapel, Cincinnati, was revitalized in 1895 by the adoption of "storehouse tithing," following Malachi 3:10-12.[38] This "covenant plan" spread among many Christians, especially Presbyterians. So did "The Tenth Legion" and "The Twentieth Century Tither's Association of America." Scholarly undergirding was given in 1906 by Dr. Henry Lansdell's two-volume work entitled *The Sacred Tenth*.[39]

There is not enough space here to go into detail about the Laymen's Missionary Movement or the leadership of Ralph S. Cushman at the Methodist Church in Geneva, New York, and its dramatic results with the tithe. Cushman later became president of the United Stewardship Council (1920-50). It was in the period around the First World War that laity came into prominence in some churches for the first time, and that in connection with fund-raising campaigns. The economic depression in the thirties dampened efforts of this sort, but the "Lord's Acre Plan" or the idea of giving your pay for the first hour's work on Monday morning to the church arose in these adverse times.[40]

3. Ecumenical Cooperation

The stewardship movement was ecumenical in many aspects.[41] Many of the efforts already described naturally cut across denominational lines. While each church body seemed to have a major but separate fund appeal, especially after World War II, there was also a growing commonality of interest in stewardship, in the sharing of statistics and even methods and content. The Joint Department of Stewardship and Benevolence of the National Council of the Churches of Christ in the U.S.A. proved especially important in these matters. Even conservative groups such as the Lutheran Church–Missouri Synod, which chose not to affiliate with a national council of churches, were open to sharing in such work about fund-raising.

Under T. K. Thompson, the NCC Department of Stewardship and Benevolence also achieved a significant plan of publication for stewardship resources. Particularly noteworthy in this regard is the Library of Christian Stewardship series, which has enlisted contributions from members of major theological faculties.[42] The partnership for ministry between academic theologians and church stewardship leaders probably peaked in the early 1960s, at least to date.

A personal example. For the annual meeting of Stewardship and Benevolence in 1961 I was invited to share my findings from my doctoral dissertation in Classical Studies on the Greek word that can be translated stewardship, namely *oikonomia*.[43] Out of that contact came an invitation to speak throughout the African Methodist Episcopal Church in the South on the theme. This was an experience in pre-Selma days, to enter a church hall on a steaming hot day in Birmingham or Jacksonville, the stage festooned with the word O-I-K-O-N-O-M-I-A in cut-out letters, and share the New Testament background and references exegetically.

4. Changed Emphases in the Sixties and Seventies

For a variety of reasons, however, the situation changed in the late 1960s and early '70s. Stewardship receded in interest among the churches and within many denominations. The chief factor was the rise of the civil rights issue in the United States and the debate over the Vietnam War. Social statements, social action, demonstrations, marches, and protest marked out new areas of attention in religious circles, among Roman Catholics and Jews as well as Protestants. Stewardship, like evangelism, was put on the back burner. This is not to say that programs in the area ceased but simply that in most denominations stewardship became somewhat old hat. Each church body had a slightly different story, and formal histories are hard to come by,[44] but the larger outline is clear: the social-action period in North American Christianity placed stewardship in the shade. When it revived as a concern, it would be with an emphasis on including precisely such matters. Indeed, its persistent ability to absorb the latest trends within itself will become apparent here.

5. New Developments in Outlook

Crucial to an understanding of the history of stewardship in the late seventies and in the eighties is an awareness of the influential role played by the NCCCUSA's Commission on Stewardship (COS) and its director, Nordan Murphy, and behind that the enlistment of Douglas John Hall by The United Church of Canada's Department of Stewardship Services. This is not to overlook numerous other persons on ecumenical and denominational church staffs, educators, clergy, and theologians who also played important roles in the reshaping of the stewardship movement; it is simply to acknowledge the very visible role of Hall's three books, which were outgrowths of sessions at COS meetings from 1978 on. These sessions served to bring stewardship into a new relationship with academia.

The overall argument in the first two of these three books by Hall is that the symbol of the steward and stewardship originated in the biblical writings but never came to fruition either in the New Testament or the early church. Hall attributes this failure to the facts that (1) in the New Testament itself apocalyptic eschatology diverted attention from this-worldly stewardship, (2) in the patristic church Hellenization led to an otherworldliness, and (3) later on, the "Constantinian establishment" set aside the mutual responsibility of Christians to serve one another and replaced it with state support and self-service and a drive for power. But the symbol of the steward, he holds, came of age in the 1970s.[45]

It was in North American Christianity that stewardship originally came into its own, says Hall, but it was usually tied to church programs of fund-raising for evangelism and world mission, emphases that today are looked upon as "triumphalistic" and "imperial." However, the good news is that the world is using stewardship as a positive concept in fresh ways — for example, in ecology.[46] So he argues that the time is ripe for a new assessment of stewardship, and specifically he suggests that the North American context allows for a liberation-theology style of indigenous praxis and reflection.

According to Hall, stewardship means a commitment to the care of this world. Our first priority should be to get rid of all ambiguity in our attitude toward this world. The theological base for Hall's program incorporates the principles of globalization, communalization, ecologization, politicization, and futurization. The invitation to stewardship entails a call to the rich nations of the world to pay more attention to Third World needs, to a theology of nature (in terms of humanity living in harmony with nature), and to peace issues, which ought to command our attention as "stewards for the blessedness of this world."[47]

Hall defines stewardship as "the whole posture called Christian," in a "stewardship of all believers." And mission thus becomes stewardship, a necessity for the world and a possibility, though at the cost of some risk, for Christians and the church.

In his 1985 volume *Christian Mission: The Stewardship of Life in the Kingdom of Death,* which is more sermonic and dialogical, Hall tackles mission more specifically. He sharpens the issues by insisting that we are living in an age of death and that the only alternative is to "choose life." He deepens the arguments presented in the previous volume, writing in the form of meditations, and concluding with answers to questions from hearers at the end of each chapter.

The third of Hall's books under consideration here, *Imaging God: Dominion as Stewardship* (1986), has more of the flavor of a systematic theology than the other two. Hall explores the concept of the *imago Dei,* speaks of the human vocation of "imaging God," and discusses the topic of human "dominion" over the rest of creation.

The COS has sponsored work in other areas, such as investigations of the socio-ethical and political aspects of stewardship and lectures on the possible relationships of stewardship with process philosophy and feminist theologies.[48] Others have touched upon innumerable aspects of practical theology. Indeed, in its concern to cover all the bases, recent stewardship discussions seem to have taken up all the so-called burning issues except that of gays and lesbians, at least to the best of my knowledge. Perhaps in time someone will launch a study on "the stewardship of sex"!

It should be noted that the ecumenical stewardship ministry begun by churches in Canada and United States in 1920 is now being done by the Ecumenical Center for Stewardship Studies (ECSS). The ECSS has its offices in Indianapolis and is related to the National Council of the Churches of Christ in the U.S.A. and to the Canadian Interchurch Stewardship Committee.

6. Some Observations

This history of stewardship studies and programs need not be evaluated here, but a few comments are in order.

a. Stewardship is by and large *North American* and *Protestant* in its origins and development. There is relatively little influence from, or reflection of, the stewardship movement in Roman Catholicism or Eastern Orthodoxy, let alone Judaism or the non-Christian religions. Salstrand began his conclusions with the statement "Stewardship has been an American contribution to theological thinking."[49] He is able to refer only to Protestant groups.

b. Throughout much of its career over more than the past century, stewardship has been *"practical"* —perhaps a characteristic American virtue. Born of the need to support ministry and missions, stewardship has been enlisted in many subsequent causes of interest to given churches and individuals at one time or another. Stewardship has not so much had a theology of its own as it has been a vast movement *in search of a theology.* Interest in relating stewardship to more systematic, constructive, or dogmatic theology and ethics has been more evident during the period from 1950 to 1965 and again during the past decade than at any other time. But stewardship has proven itself capable of alliances with Calvinism, Methodism, the Episcopal outlook, Lutheran theology, Baptist emphases, Protestant liberalism, conservative evangelicalism, and all the trends of the 1980s.

c. There is relatively *little evidence of denominational distinctives* in stewardship literature and approaches. Salstrand explored the subject in the context of ten larger and twelve smaller denominations, and the story is remarkably the same in each.[50] This is not to suggest that the various communions fail to give stewardship their own unique emphases — Methodist groups stressing sanctification, for example, or Lutherans stressing justification, or Presbyterians stressing God's sovereignty behind the divine plan — but in the end a commonality of idiom overrides the denominational distinctives in the context of stewardship.

d. Shall we make anything of this commonality with regard to *ecumenism?* Is there de facto some sort of agreement among the churches that obtains here, to which no ecumenical statement of which I know makes any allusion? (The reference is only to relationships among Protestants here, since stewardship is not a Catholic or Eastern Orthodox theme.) Or is there a cleft between law orientations and grace orientations that establishes a dividing line?

e. In any event, we are left with the essential *dilemma* of whether stewardship is merely a matter of fund-raising or is a much broader, all-embracing matter.

Surely Hall's proposals have been the most far-reaching ever. In his enthusiasm for stewardship, he has made a daring move with regard to mission; it has been redefined (some would say out of existence). He rejects church growth in terms of membership, at least through conversions, as "imperialist."[51] He theologically justifies his assertion that "smaller is better" for churches with appeals to a "theology of the cross."[52] He prefers to understand mission as a matter of cooperating with all people of goodwill on ecological matters. All this could have structural implications for any denomination. Organizations devoted to global and domestic mission work would have to be relocated under the office of stewardship in the denominational structure. As a matter of church politics, such a shift is so unlikely as not to be worth discussing, but it reflects a trend that NCC studies have clearly endorsed theologically.

In 1980 Nordan Murphy put the matter in terms of his own personal experience, as follows:

> When Christian stewardship first emerged as a Biblical and theological concept which I considered worthy of my personal consideration it had a very minuscule meaning.
>
> Stewardship was identified with fundraising. This expanded to a consideration of the use of one's time and talents. Further expansion included all of one's money, not just that

60

portion given to worthy causes (the Church being either the only, or most worthy), but how one uses 100 percent of his/her financial power. Later, stewardship understanding for me addressed the subject of corporate responsibility: daring to challenge the manner in which the congregation and the institutions of the Church exercised trusteeship in the collective funds, facilities, and human resources at their disposal.

In the early '60s, we started to realize that the Psalmist was correct, "The earth is the Lord's and the fullness thereof," and that the subject was relevant for Christian stewardship study. Biblical and theological papers and reflections upon truths, unearthed thereby, started to disturb the serious stewardship student.

Impacted by the emergence of our racial and ethnic prejudices, stewardship students explored more deeply the scriptural interpretation of liberation theologians. Truly, the "whole creation has been groaning in travail" (Rom 8:22). *Stewardship is the liberating theological concept for the earth and the whole of its inhabitants.*[53]

f. Finally, and more controversially, the history of stewardship shows that it is highly *susceptible to* the particular *interests of the day* and the current passions of individual theologians or church administrative staff.

We are all creatures of our own time. When church leaders, pastors, or theologians are asked to do something for a particular denomination or the Commission on Stewardship ecumenically, they draw, almost inevitably, on their own experiences and what they have been working on, on their graduate dissertation topics or whatever they might be researching at the moment (myself included, as a prime example). All this is perhaps inevitable, and at times it may even be productive. But we must ask whether we have not made stewardship into an umbrella term, to cover our own personal interests or the social or other trends of the day. Is there anything in the nature of stewardship itself, beyond fundraising, that identifies core themes, suggests directions, or sets limits? The chapters above have sought to do that by tracing the history of the term that stands behind "stewardship" in the New Testament and early Christianity. Studies in the economy of God provide parameters. It is now time to apply this heritage, in light of growing secular use of the term, to the stewardship of the future.

Vantage Points in History and Theology for Reuniting Stewardship and the Economy of God

Left to its own devices, stewardship, that less than two-centuries-old North American contribution to Christianity, need mean nothing more than fund-raising pure and simple. Or it can extend itself into an all-encompassing, even pretentious, expression that overarches all Christian life and faith.

Defined as Douglas John Hall would have it, stewardship is a biblical symbol that has come of age only in North America. Even the New Testament never quite got it right. It means care of the globe, together with all right-minded, ecologically inclined people, and correct political action for the future of society. The price for such a definition is to write off almost all church history and presumably most theologizing from Constantine the Great until contemporary liberation theology and seemingly to give up evangelism, which converts people to Jesus Christ, as presumptuous. In Nordan Murphy's phrase, "stewardship is the liberating theological concept for the earth and the whole of its inhabitants."[1]

The economy of God is a theme some two thousand years old. Employed by Greeks and Romans, it referred to the divine and prudential ordering of the world and all life. As developed by Christians, it came to mean the acts of God seen supremely in the incarnation, death, and resurrection of Jesus, as well as earlier in the creation and throughout Israel's history, and subsequently in the lives of Christians, the history of the church, and the course of the world. Yet this "grand design" has fallen on hard times, and nowadays people even in the churches know only bits and pieces of the epic whole.

There is something right and something wrong about each of the three paragraphs above. The first asks, What *is* Christian stewardship? The second seeks to extend the concept to all people in the world. The third wrestles with God's reign and plan in history and in human lives.

Is there a way to unite what is good and helpful in these various understandings of stewardship and the divine economy on a firm biblical and theological base? After all, the same Greek vocabulary lies behind "steward" and "stewardship" on the one hand and New Testament references to God's plan or management of the world and of salvation on the other — namely, *oikonomia* terminology.

The challenge to take the grand narrative about God's will and work to create, deliver, and recreate and put it together with stewardship as a response concerning faithful use of our resources is made both pressing and opportune by conditions in the world today, as is well known, and by voices that bring new attention to each theme.

In recent times a new desire to lift up the biblical narrative, the great Christian story of salvation, from beginning to end, has arisen among theologians, biblical scholars, preachers, educators, and people in the pews. The late Hans Frei, of Yale, who lamented the "eclipse" of this biblical narrative, called for reappropriation of its epic sweep, including the continuation in the church, as developed by Augustine, Luther, and Calvin.[2] George Lindbeck has endorsed the proposal and specified how telling this story lies at the heart of the Christian enterprise and its roots in Israel.[3]

Gabriel Fackre has set his hand to producing a three-volume systematic theology around this story-line.[4] Narrative theology is the new vogue in biblical exegesis. Brevard Childs has emphasized the significance of the canonical norm and the interplay of the books in the Bible with each other for biblical theology and the church.[5] In these and other efforts we see a new emphasis on the cohesiveness of the biblical and subsequent Christian story about a God who spoke and speaks, who acted and acts, who planned and executes a design to rule in righteousness and mercifully deliver.

Over the last decade or so, there has also been a resuscitation of the word "stewardship." It was not only the practice of Christian stewardship that went into decline in many churches in the seventies but even the word itself. "Steward" was relegated to the scrap heap. While Hall's books brought the term back into prominence (albeit redefined) in some ecumenical circles, it was really a rediscovery by journalists and society in general that elevated stewardship into a new and somewhat different prominence.

People all over have now begun to use the term "stewardship" quite apart from church or Christianity, in the sense of "responsible use of resources" or wise management of what is at one's disposal. To cite almost random examples from the New York *Times* alone, there were in 1986 and 1987 references to "concern about the stewardship of America's great corporate bureaucracies," "Mrs. Thatcher's economic stewardship" in Great Britain, Mayor Koch's "first steps toward redeeming his stewardship" in New York City after a scandal, the head of the U.S. Internal Revenue Service ending "the longest stewardship of any commissioner since World War II," and even the "stewardship of tradition" in baseball exercised by the clubhouse attendant of the New York Yankees. In the 1991 financial news we read that "stewardship of the $16 billion Fidelity Magellan Fund, the nation's largest stock fund, changed hands last year." You don't have to be in church work to use stewardship language!

In facing the challenge to reunite the divine economy and stewardship, we might proceed in terms of "God talk." M. Douglas Meeks has attempted such a program in a book entitled *God the Economist*.[6] Or one could, as Hall's *Imaging God* suggests, give attention to the *imago Dei*, or "image of God," in human beings and thus to "anthropology," or the human situation and makeup. Here two biblical pictures emerge in the narrative. (1) All humanity, God says, is made "in the image of God," "after our likeness" (Gen. 1:26, 27); this image, though undefined in the Bible and defaced in the disobedience recorded in Genesis 3 and subsequent sinning, is never lost. Genesis 5:1-3 reports that, just as "God created humankind . . . in the likeness of God," so Adam "became the father of a son in his own likeness, according to his image" (NRSV), and so on down the line. (2) Paul suggests that Jesus Christ is in a unique way "the image of the invisible God" (Col. 1:15) and that only when united with Christ through baptism does a person become clothed with "the new self, which is being renewed . . . according to the image of its creator" (Col. 3:10, NRSV). These double references compel one to think of (1) all human beings as having an image of God by nature, even if defaced (some would say destroyed), and of (2) those in Christ as alone possessing the image of God and being renewed on the way to its fullness through being incorporated into Christ.[7] Or, in addition to the themes of God-talk and the *imago Dei*, one could attempt to revive stewardship along the lines of some particular confessional or denominational themes; the doctrine of justification and citations from Martin Luther, for example,[8] or the doctrine of election and citations from John Calvin.

In our survey of the economy-of-God theme, we have seen that the concept has frequently been intertwined with a view of history, an understanding of how God's plan or stewardship unfolded historically in Israel, in Jesus, and in the early and subsequent church. Usually the heart of the matter has been seen to reside in certain seminal events that are regarded as decisive for knowing what God is about and for effecting a new or "saved" relationship of *shalom* with God. These insights could be projected forward, beyond the Christ event, in the history of the whole Christian movement as well as in the day-to-day existence of individual believers. They could likewise be attested in prior history and traced back to the very beginning of things, at the creation.

That "God works toward a goal" is one way of putting the underlying principle that is assumed in the economy of God. Most understandings of stewardship tacitly or openly rest upon such an understanding too, whether the goal is "the social gospel made flesh," "partnership with Christ" or God, the service of others, uniting people to the church, advancement of Christ's mission, management of God-given resources, or liberation of the earth and its inhabitants.

At issue is where to start and what to emphasize in the story of God's working in the world "for us and for our salvation" and then how to relate the divine economy to all the various conceptions of stewardship. We shall proceed by looking at divine activity from the perspective of three different points in time. Then in Chapter V we will explore the ways in which stewardship and the divine economy can be related in accord with these three vantage points.

A. Ways to Approach How God Works in History toward a Goal

By now it is clear that Christians have entertained a considerable variety of attitudes about history — historical and systematic theologians especially but also average members of congregations. Are there ways to classify, and so discuss, how God may work toward whatever goal we assume to be the aim of the divine plan or stewardship in historical events? Three basic ways in which Christians have looked at history may be proposed, three basic perspectives associated with different starting points for laying hold of the work of centuries, points at which it can be said that God definitely was involved or acted in events that serve to clarify the divine intent for us and for the world. They amount to looking at history from the beginning, the middle, or the end. In each is stressed a portion of the statement "God works toward a goal."

1. Beginnings (ab initio)

One venerable way to look at history is from its start. That is the way canonical Scripture commences — "In the beginning God created . . ." (Gen. 1:1). Such is the way the fourth Gospel initiates its theological prologue — "In the beginning was the Word" (John 1:1). It is a line of argument Jesus used about marriage — "From the beginning of creation, 'God made them male and female'" (Mark 10:6). *Ab initio* is the Latin in the Vulgate rendering of this passage. The implication can be either "So it was in the beginning, but look how you've corrupted it" or "So it was in the beginning, and thus things have unfolded ever since, in accord with these beginnings."

Such a way of thinking, *ab initio,* is not confined to Christians, of course. Judaism reckons its calendar to this day from the creation, the date based on totaling up subsequent biblical chronologies, so that 1992 of the Common Era (C.E.) is for Jews the year 5753 since creation. Ancient Rome, we noted, reckoned events "A.U.C," *ab urbe condita,* "from the founding of the city" of Rome, traditionally in 753 B.C. by our chronology.

Theologically, this approach to history lays great emphasis on the doctrine of creation. As in Genesis 1, God spoke, it happened, and it was good. That account could lead to a powerful theology of the word and an affirmation of the world and its history. Or, if one begins with Genesis 2 and 3, those chapters portray human beings as rebels, yet God as one who succors them even in discipline (3:21).

All views of the world and history that start with beginnings stress the power and sovereignty of God. There is often an emphasis on Providence continuing after creation along the path of history, and there may be a note of predestination or election: God accepts Abel, not Cain; in Israel's epic, Yahweh follows with blessing the descendants of Shem, through Abraham, Isaac, Jacob, and Joseph, but not Esau and his line. Put in a word, this approach stresses *God,* the subject in the statement "*God* works toward a goal."

If we look in the history of theology for interpreters who viewed the world and its history *ab initio,* we have not only the biblical writers including the Yahwist (J) and the Priestly writer(s) (P) but later on also certain schools of theology. In the seventeenth and eighteenth centuries, the Deists in England and elsewhere provide a prominent example; they saw God as "the great Clockmaker" who had started the whole contraption going and then retired. Another group is exemplified by Calvin, who stressed the divine Sovereign's rule and did theology from the perspective of God in heaven. Some of those who view history from the perspective of its beginnings see a grand design in operation from the outset. Among the pagans, the Stoic philosophers envisioned an endless cycle of flux and reflux, like the legendary phoenix, dying to revive again. Among Christians, a ladder might be a more fitting symbol — Jacob's ladder (Gen. 28:12), for example, reaching to the Eternal City of God.[9] John Smith, the Cambridge Platonist, put it thus in 1660:

> To a superficial observer of *Divine Providence* many things there are that seem to be nothing else but *Digressions* from the main End of all. . . . But a wise man that looks from the Beginning to the End of things, beholds them all in their due place and method acting that part which the Supreme Mind and Wisedome that governs all things hath appointed them, and to carry on one and the same Eternal designe.[10]

There thus can be stewardships of history, theology, and life that take their clue from the Beginning.

2. *The Middle of History (in medias res)*

Other interpretations of history take their clue, however, from some key event in the midst of history. We may designate this approach with the phrase *in medias res,* "in the middle of things." That is how some stories start — Virgil's *Aeneid,* for example — in the middle of the action. Then follow flashbacks about what has transpired before, and interspersed with these are events that follow. In a way, that is how Israel's tale unfolded. Surely at the heart of that people's faith was the exodus from Egypt. As the experiences in the wilderness, at Sinai, and then the conquest followed, faith also looked back to experiences of the patriarchs and even projected itself to the beginning of the world to speak about creation.

New Testament faith was centered in the death and resurrection of Jesus. That key event became the focal point for writing in the epistles about the expected fulfillment in the future and about the present and new meaning of life between Easter and the parousia. Faith also looked back over Jesus' life and retold the story of his ministry in the Gospels from the standpoint of the time of the exalted Lord, after Easter. Christians further reread Israel's history as now also their own. They made assertions concerning the creation in a way that gave Jesus Christ a decisive role as God's vicegerent at the foundation of the world. A letter by Paul finds its heart in "Christ crucified and risen." But in light of Christ, the apostle may also speak of Israel in the wilderness (1 Cor. 10:1-10), Christ at creation (1 Cor. 8:6; cf. Col. 1:15-20), the last judgment (2 Cor. 5:10), and Christ's lordship over all our lives (Rom. 14:8-9).

We have seen an illustration of this approach at work in the chronological system of B.C. ("before Christ") and A.D. (*anno Domini,* "in the year of the Lord"). It places the Christ event at the very center of universal history. The Puritan divine Jonathan Edwards wrote of how Christian theology, in whole and in each part, stands in reference to "the great work of redemption by

70

Jesus Christ," which he calls "the grand design of God," so that "the body of divinity" is cast "in an entire new method, being thrown into the form of a history."[11]

There are many familiar theological emphases associated with this view of history, among them christocentricity, *theologia crucis* (the "theology of the cross," stressing "Christ crucified"), a sense of divine presence, and incarnational theology.

If the emphasis of the *ab initio* perspective is evident in the expression "*God* works toward a goal," the emphasis of the *in medias res* perspective is evident in the expression "God *works* toward a goal." Indeed, those who adopt this perspective perceive God to be working here and now. Of course, the supreme example and definitive moment for understanding all of God's activity is what occurred in and through Jesus of Nazareth.

All theologies of *Heilsgeschichte* fit here, including that of Oscar Cullmann, to take a prominent example.[12] Many patristic theologies can be classified here too. Often the early Christian writers spoke of continuing interpositions of God's saving power in their own day, in light of what they had come to know in Jesus Christ. So too most theologies involving experience with God's presence and power belong in this category, as God continues to work in light of the supreme revelation through Christ.

3. The End (de novissima)

Last of all there is the approach to a theology of history that looks at things from the vantage point of the end — the end of the world, the denouement of history, the standpoint of fulfillment, in light of that day when all will be made new and the peaceable kingdom will bask in God's *shalom,* when God's purposes will finally and fully have been carried through, for good.

While this aspect for doing theology may seem to be in its outlook "apocalyptic" — to use what for some has become a "dirty word," the trademark of millenarian sects — the fact is that the futurist approach extends well beyond what even so elastic a term as "apocalyptic" covers. A number of other schools of theology can be classified here. I have chosen the Latin phrase *de novissima* to point to this larger range of meaning. The phrase turns up in old manuals of theology as the title for the locus or section on "eschatology." It means, literally, "concerning the newest things." That is really what eschatology and even apocalyptic literature and thought are about — not simply "the last things" but the "latest things" that God is doing, the newest good news, indeed that at the End. Where the *ab initio* perspective stresses that "*God* works toward a goal," and the *in medias res* perspective stresses that "God *works* toward a goal," the *de novissima* perspective stresses that "God works *toward a goal.*"

A theology of history from this angle looks at events not from the eye of God at the beginning or from some key happening centuries ago but in light of what will be. In some forms of apocalyptic thinking, we see history unfolding toward the New Jerusalem or toward that moment described in 1 Thessalonians 4:17, when dead and living saints will be caught up to be with Christ in what was in the nineteenth century termed "the rapture." The umbrella term "apocalyptic" thus includes, for better or worse, even the designs created by Hal Lindsey and a host like him who speculate on the exact sequence of the events leading up to "the End."

But also under this banner of "the End" one must put the Pannenberg School, Jürgen Moltmann, and all "theologies of hope."[13] It is sometimes forgotten that the Pannenberg circle began with emphasis on revelation as history in light of the expected end, apocalyptically: in Christ's resurrection we catch a glimpse of the firstfruits. To say "God is the power of the future" is to cast even our definition of God not *ab initio* or in terms of past event but in light of the fulfillment, when God will be all in all. Teilhard de Chardin, process theology, and all notions of God evolving and an "omega point" fit here.

Obviously, future-oriented theologies that look at history in light of the End, in all their variety, have proven immensely popular in recent years. But the hard-nosed historian will have to ask why. Is this a cop-out, an attempt to remove God from beginnings and all debate about creation, to set aside messy disputes about whether God acts in history (and, if so, which happenings are to be assigned to God)? The *de novissima* perspective pushes God into the future, where we can neither falsify nor verify what God will be like at the end.

B. Summary

More will be said later about these three perspectives on the activity of God in history, but it suffices at this point to suggest that each of them is a valid expression of Christian faith. God's work and plan may be viewed from three vantage points:

at the beginning of things	from a central point in history	from the end of all things.

Each of these perspectives concentrates on certain themes:

the creation of the world and of humanity	Israel's exodus, Jesus' cross and resurrection, the incarnation	the Day of the Lord, the parousia and judgment.

Each can be summed up in a word,

"Protology" — the doctrine of first things	Christology — the work and person of Christ	"Teleology" — the doctrine of last things.

It is possible to find among Old Testament historians examples of each of these approaches:

Second Isaiah	the Yahwist (J)	apocalyptists
(ab initio)	*(in medias res)*	*(de novissima).*

All of these approaches thus have biblical foundations, precedent, and examples. They simply function in and address different situations.

It is possible, of course, to try to bring all of these witnesses together in one grand presentation of "the view of history in the Hebrew Scriptures." Such an undertaking is the task of Old Testament theology.[14]

What of the New Testament? The earliest followers of Jesus, both during his lifetime and after Easter, were Jews who would have been familiar with at least some of these views from the Bible of their day. But at Easter a new factor entered or was at least reinforced. Ernst Käsemann has termed the apocalyptic mood touched off by the resurrection of Jesus (for how could one hear that "God has raised Jesus from the dead" without expecting all the events of the "last days" soon to follow?) to be "the mother of Christ theology."[15] That is to say, Christians first theologized in an apocalyptic, eschatological key. In time, as the gospel moved outside Palestine to the Hellenistic world and as Jews from the diaspora or who had familiarity with Hellenistic culture (such as Josephus, Philo, or Paul, all did) became active in the Jesus movement, their ways of telling the story about Jesus and its meanings began to reflect the historical techniques of the Greco-Roman world.

Of course, all the New Testament witnesses can be put together into a composite "view of history in the New Testament writings." That is the task of New Testament theology.[16] Eventually there was an increasing Hellenization of Christianity, which became evident in christology, in accounts of the creation, and even with regard to the world and its eventual destiny, to say nothing of concepts of history. Here the heritage of Polybius, Diodorus Siculus, and Greek historians and philosophers proved to be of great importance to the Church Fathers, with the result that "biblical theology" was often constructed on the framework provided by such ideas as "the economy *(oikonomia)* of God." But — a cautionary note — the starting point for New Testament and all Christian developments, as we will see in Chapter V, was the way of thinking mentioned last in the account above of Old Testament approaches — namely, the apocalyptic mind-set. It must not be minimalized.

How, now, can these three vantage points for comprehending history be related to stewardship?

Three Approaches to Stewardship within the Economy of God

What do we wish to make of stewardship today? What can be said of it, given its long history of hanging somewhere between "mere fund-raising" — a perfectly honorable necessity in any organization's life — and pretensions to all sorts of theological range and scope?

All of our options are problematic. If we choose to equate stewardship with mere fund-raising, we will still have to establish the philosophy behind it and a permissible methodology. Is the guiding star to be "self-sacrifice," as in the story of the widow's mite (if that is what Mark 12:41-44 really means),[1] or the theology of indulgences, such as were sold by John Tetzel, patron saint of all ruthless, organization-minded fund-raisers? If stewardship involves theology and ethics, *which* theology? *whose* ethics? and with *what concept* of God's mission? Furthermore, how can creation be brought in? Can creation and history be confined simply to the past? What of the eschatological, indeed futurist outlook? Is apocalyptic the menace some believe it to be, or is it a necessary constituent to a proper biblical outlook and for stewardship today?

We begin with what may be the most obvious area among these possibilities, a staunchly traditional one — salvation history. It involves a theme to which many in the discussions of the National Council of Churches Joint Department of Stewardship and Benevolence in the 1950s and '60s would instantly have resonated. But it is a facet of biblical interpretation and a concept in theology generally that has gone into something of an eclipse. What can be said of it in light of past studies and the situation today?

A. Stewardship as the History of Salvation and Our Role within the Economy of God

The translation of the German term *Heilsgeschichte* into English has itself given rise to dispute. It is typically translated "salvation history" or "redemptive history," but that does not mean that "history saves" or "redeems," for God does.[2] "Holy history," another, even less fortunate phrase, has sometimes been employed, but this draws fire for implying that there is also "unholy" history. Even Alan Richardson's phrase "history sacred and profane" can be misleading.[3]

What is meant by "salvation history" is that in certain events within human history, such as Jesus' cross and resurrection, God can with special clarity be seen working to save. The German word *Heilsgeschichte* is helpful at times to suggest this sense. While one can claim a long prior history and certain antecedents to *Heilsgeschichte* — going back at least to Irenaeus and the "grand design" that Christians saw in history for some eighteen centuries[4] — the concept of this sort of salvation history arose amid quite specific conditions in Germany during the last century.

1. Nineteenth-Century Historicism and the Theology of Heilsgeschichte

It is worth reminding ourselves that modern, scientific historiography arose only in the nineteenth century. The Renaissance and Enlightenment emphasis on interrogating the sources was at this time refined into increasingly precise techniques in order to discover what really had happened in the past. The aim was "real history," and only history was considered real. History had become god, as Johann Tobias Beck of Tübingen put it. The old days, as when J. A. Bengel, the south German pietist, traced out God's economy in his sage comments on the New Testament, had come to an end. Now was the time of Hegelian analysis, of Ferdinand Christian Baur's reconstruction of Christian origins, when David Friedrich Strauss laid rough hands on the historical Jesus.[5]

But the Tübingen School of theology, as the approach of Baur, Strauss, and others became known, was not the only option. At another south German university arose what became known as "Erlangen theology,"[6] and to many it proved far more wholesome. It sought a synthesis of history and salvation for theology and Christian life through a system marked by the subjective starting point of our salvation "in Christ," an objective view of God's actions, and an emphasis on the Bible as a whole rather than as a compendium of proof texts. The writings of J. C. K. von Hofmann were influential in spreading such views.[7] This salvation-history approach was later taken up by the systematician Martin Kähler and the New Testament and systematics scholar Adolf Schlatter. The latter's lexicographic interests helped give birth to Gerhard Kittel's monumental *Theological Dictionary of the New Testament,* many articles in which have a clearly *heilsgeschichtlich* orientation.

2. Oscar Cullmann

The great champion of *Heilsgeschichte* in more recent times has been the Swiss New Testament professor Oscar Cullmann. While Cullmann has sought to distance his work from that of the Erlangen School in order to make a fresh beginning on his own, many see a lineal relationship, above all in the term *Heils-*

geschichte and the pun Cullmann makes on it in his 1965 work *Heil als Geschichte*, "salvation as history," and a reference in the subtitle to *heilsgeschichtlich* existence.[8]

For our purposes it is most important to note how Cullmann relates his view of *Heilsgeschichte* to *oikonomia*. He took up the term from Paul and used it to refer, as the "economy of God," to a "continuous redemptive line" running through all history. It is a little hard to know how to translate *oikonomia (tou theou)* here, whether as "God's economy" or "God's stewardship" or "the divine redemptive plan and purpose." Cullmann simply uses the Greek word. On this redemptive line running through time — and it must be recalled that he titled his chief book *Christ and Time: The Primitive Christian Conception of Time and History*[9] — Cullmann placed a number of *x*'s to denote moments when God had been particularly active. Each *x* he called a *kairos,* the Greek term for a particularly significant "time" or moment in history. The term can be found in Mark 1:15 in Jesus' proclamation that "the time [*ho kairos*] is fulfilled." Examples of *kairoi* on the *oikonomia* line of God through time would include preeminently the exodus of Israel out of Egypt and, in a broad, summary term, the "Christ event." That "event" could, in turn, be broken down into a series of smaller or larger *x*'s specifying, for example, Jesus' baptism, transfiguration, crucifixion, and, above all, incarnation. As we have seen, the Church Fathers used *oikonomia* to refer to each of these significant happenings in history. See Chart II on page 81 for a visual representation of Cullmann's thought.

Cullmann expanded on this basic idea of an *oikonomia* line marked by *kairoi* moments with his observation that there is a movement "from the Many to the One" in the Old Testament, a process of selection that results in a shift in focus from all humanity first to Israel and then to a remnant within the chosen people. In the New Testament, he argues, this movement is reversed: the Christ event initiates a shift in focus "from the One to the Many." The imagery comes from Romans 5:18 ("as one man's trespass led to condemnation for all, so one man's act of righteousness

CHART II: SALVATION HISTORY (HEILSGESCHICHTE) AS DEVELOPED BY OSCAR CULLMANN

A. Two Greek Terms Employed as Basic Concepts:

—— = *oikonomia,* the time line

x = *kairoi,* significant events in God's work of salvation

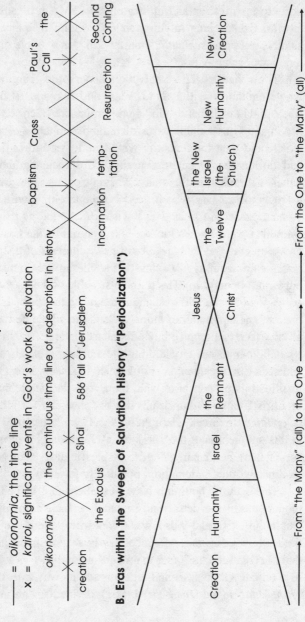

B. Eras within the Sweep of Salvation History ("Periodization")

leads to justification and life for all," NRSV) and Jesus' saying at Mark 10:45 about his life being a ransom for many, as well as other passages such as 1 Timothy 2:6 (Jesus "gave himself as a ransom for all").

The broad sweep of salvation history thus runs from the whole creation (Gen. 1–2) to Adam and Eve and all humanity (Gen. 2–11) to Israel as God's chosen people (Gen. 12 through 2 Kings 17) and finally to a dwindling remnant — Judah, the exiles, and then the few who were true to God after the return and during the Maccabean period. This focusing movement, which Cullmann pictures as a V lying on its side, eventually narrows to just One who is entirely true to God's will and plan — namely, Jesus Christ. The Jewish leaders, all the people, and even his own disciples forsake him. But out of the Easter event grows an ever-increasing series of new segments of people. This is depicted again as a V lying on its side but this time directed outward, opening up. The segments include "the twelve," who correspond to the Old Testament remnant; the "new Israel," or church; and finally all of humanity and the whole new creation, all of which has a place in God's plan.

Cullmann's view of a time-line and salvation history is, of course, a Christ-centered view of the divine *oikonomia.* Cullmann justifies this by appeal to what the Epistle to the Hebrews says of Christ's coming and death: it was "once and for all" (*hapax* or *ephapax* in Greek, Heb. 9:26, 28; cf. 9:12; 10:10). He refers to this uniqueness of the Christ event, Jesus and his cross, as the "scandal of particularity." In this specific Jew from Nazareth, God has worked redemption, potentially for all.

This way of outlining New Testament and indeed biblical thought has had its detractors, especially in the Bultmann School. But in the 1950s and '60s it was a widespread method of treating the Bible. Cullmann's influence may be responsible for the fact that "heilsgeschichte" as a loanword in English (without italics or a telltale German capital letter) made its way into *Webster's Third Unabridged Dictionary* (1961), defined as "an interpretation of history emphasizing God's saving acts and viewing Jesus Christ as central in redemption."

3. Vatican II, Other Examples, and the Reaction

Cullmann's version of heilsgeschichte also proved congenial in many Roman Catholic circles. The Latin phrase with which it often came to be equated, *mysterium salutis*, or "the mystery of salvation," had a significant history of its own. The concept, expressed in Latin but reflecting some of Cullmann's exegetical and ecumenical work, proved particularly important at the Second Vatican Council. Cullmann himself, it should not be forgotten, was an observer and honored guest at the Council in Rome. He did not represent any specific church or denomination but was a sort of Protestant reflection of the *una sancta*, the "one, holy" church, and proved to be in some ways a *praeceptor ecclesiae*, or teacher of the church.

The German theologian Geiko Müller-Fahrenholz has sought to trace out the quest for the economy of God in modern discussions within the World Council of Churches, Cullmann's work, and such Vatican II decrees as *Dei Verbum* ("Dogmatic Constitution on Divine Revelation"), *Lumen Gentium* ("Dogmatic Constitution on the Church"), *Unitatis Redintegratio* ("Decree on Ecumenism"), and *Nostra Aetate* ("Declaration on the Relationship of the Church to Non-Christian Religions").[10] It is possible to claim that in the mid-1960s Cullmann's brand of heilsgeschichte came close to becoming an official, dominant ecumenical theology among some Protestants and in certain Roman Catholic documents.

In the 1970s, however, theologies of heilsgeschichte receded, as did the stewardship movement in America, before other concerns, often political, for justice, peace, and ecology. There is an interesting reflection of this in the history of the Ecumenical Institute at Tantur, near Bethlehem, south of Jerusalem. It was established after Vatican II in Jordan as a place where the Cullmannian theology of salvation history might be further explored ecumenically. A number of changes have occurred since 1972, however, that have caused shifts in Tantur's program goals. Not least among these changes was the virtual demise of heilsgeschichte as an operative theology.

We have focused here especially on Cullmann as the most prominent proponent of heilsgeschichte who relates it clearly also to the Greek word for stewardship. But there are others who have developed an approach to the topic of salvation history in different ways, avoiding some of the features for which Cullmann has been criticized, such as his concept of time. Otto A. Piper of Princeton Seminary was one such scholar, well versed in the history of heilsgeschichte theology.[11] For other approaches, see *History Sacred and Profane,* by Anglican Alan Richardson; *Salvation History: A Biblical Interpretation,* by British Baptist Eric C. Rust; and *Redemption and Historical Reality,* by Isaac Rottenberg, a Presbyterian pastor. Although there are reasons for dissenting from Cullmann's view that *oikonomia* is the New Testament word for *Heilsgeschichte,* all must grant that in the writings of the Church Fathers *oikonomia* came to mean that very thing frequently.[12]

Whatever the final verdict — and in recent years the attitude toward such views of heilsgeschichte has often been one of benign neglect, if not downright ignorance about it — Cullmann staked out the striking claim that *oikonomia* provides a key ingredient for a Christian view of history and for the self-understanding of Christians. From the continuing time-line, for which Christ is the midpoint, and from the New Testament understanding of believers as stewards, the work of the church and life of the individual believer can be seen to fit into God's *oikonomia.* We derive our real significance from being part of the divine plan, stewardship, and mission.

4. The Biblical Data

Certain scriptural passages and the Bible as a whole have been part of a long debate over salvation history, for there has been and continues to be dispute about how much of Scripture can be termed heilsgeschichte. In part, of course, any answer depends on how the term is defined. But the flip side is that the very contents and nature of certain books of the Bible constantly drive the interpreter back to the issue of salvation history in Scripture. Does not the Deuteronomist (D), to take one Old Testament example, have a quite clear picture of God at work in Israel's history, on the basis of which D makes judgments concerning kings, prophets, priests, and events?[13] The whole realm of "canonical criticism" — of what results when J, E, P, and D are combined into books and we examine the completed documents and then go on to raise the further question of relations among these books or "intercanonicity" — seems to pose the topic of a salvation history afresh.[14]

Here we shall focus on two portions of the New Testament with respect to which the debate about salvation history has been lively and the dividing lines relatively clear. At issue is not merely the occurrence of such words as *oikonomia* but also concepts of history, the covenant, seminal figures in God's plan, and an understanding of mission and vocation, promise and fulfillment.

a. *Luke-Acts,* as a two-volume work, is commonly conceded to present not only Hellenistic historiography but also a theology of heilsgeschichte.

In these two volumes Luke takes up the subject of God working through Jesus (Acts 2:22) and then in the early church through the Spirit in a way that reflects Hellenistic historiography. As has often been noted, the prefaces (Luke 1:1-4; Acts 1:1-5), the speeches or sermons in Acts, and the good Greek style all suggest a writer who knew how to write history for a Greek audience. Luke might even have been aware of the approach of Polybius as he wrote — not about Rome's rise to power but about "the things that have been accomplished among us," the believers (Luke 1:1), in the days of Caesar Augustus (2:1), the emperors Tiberius (3:1), Claudius (Acts 11:28), and Nero, and their governors, in Palestine and the eastern provinces of the Empire, concluding with Rome itself.

Nowhere does Luke use the word *historia,* nor does he call himself a steward. Rather, he calls his work a "narrative" (Luke 1:1), and he calls his predecessors "ministers of the word" *(hypēretai;* cf. Diodorus Siculus, "ministers of divine Providence," *hypourgoi tēs theias pronoias).*[15] Moreover, there are difficulties associated with classifying Luke as a historian — namely, possible historical inaccuracies in his books. For example, did Jesus heal Simon Peter's mother-in-law before he called him to discipleship as Luke has it (4:38-39; 5:10-11), or afterward, as Mark has it (1:16-18, 30-31)? Why is the sequence of the rebels Theudas and Judas the Galilean mentioned in Acts 5:36-37 the reverse of what Josephus reports (*Antiquities* 20.5.1-2 = 5.97-102)? Was the "Italian cohort" stationed in Caesarea circa A.D. 38, as Luke claims (Acts 10:1)? In view of such examples, Paul J. Achtemeier has argued that Luke's famous preface to his two volumes in Luke 1:1-4 should not be read as promising a *chronological* order of events but a sequence of a different kind.[16] What kind of order?

In the opening verses of his Gospel, Luke states that he stands in succession to (1) "eyewitnesses" (the first generation of Christians, according to Achtemeier) and (2) the "ministers of the word" (the second generation) who "delivered" this narrative to "us" (a third generation). Luke's own task was to compile *(anatassein)* his narrative as "an orderly account" *(kathexēs)* so that Theophilus as reader might recognize the truth of what he had heard. But by "orderly" Luke appears to mean first of all "in a geographical sequence." The Gospel reports first on activity in Galilee (Luke 3–9:50), then a travel section through Samaria and surrounding areas (9:51–19:27), and finally in Jerusalem (19:28–24:53). Acts begins in Jerusalem (1:1–8:1; see 1:8 for the sequence), moves through Judea and Samaria (8:2–12:25), and then goes beyond, to Greece and Rome (13–28).

But there is more. The term *kathexēs* has a different meaning in Acts 11:4 than it does in Luke 1:3; in the Acts passage it has more the sense of "systematically" than "orderly" (though again, not a *chronological* order). The verse describes how, when a delegation came from Jerusalem, Peter "began and explained to them *in order*" (NEB, "the facts as they had happened"; NRSV, "step by step"). Luke goes on to offer a second account of Peter's description of the events that led to the conversion of Cornelius (11:4-17). This version is not presented in the same way (indeed, the sequence of events is not even given in the same order) as the original narrative in 10:9-33. And yet in 11:4, Luke says that Peter explained things to the people in Jerusalem "in order." This must mean "in an appropriate way," as Achtemeier puts it, "in a given literary (rather than historical) order."[17]

The suggestion that Luke wrote not in a chronological order but in a way appropriate to the subject at hand bears some similarity to the famous description of the "order" of Mark's Gospel made by Papias in the second century. Of Mark's Gospel this bishop of Hierapolis said, Mark "wrote accurately, but not in order [*ou mentoi taxei*] the things either said or done by the Lord," fitting his discourses "to the needs" of his hearers.[18] It would be attractive to think that Papias had in mind a contrast found in the rhetoricians: *taxis* (what Mark lacks) means chronological order; the contrasting term is *oikonomia,* "strategic order," or sequence to meet the appropriate needs of a case.[19] In any event, if Luke wrote "appropriately arranged" history, the question remains, arranged in accord with what?

Luke's arrangement of material in both his Gospel and Acts is dictated not only by the sources at his disposal but also by the theology of heilsgeschichte with which he operated. There is considerable agreement that his thought was structured around the idea of three eras: (1) the Age of Israel; (2) the "Time of Jesus," a unique period when the Savior was on earth; and (3) the Age of the Church, the period after Jesus' resurrection and ascension and the day of Pentecost. The centerpiece for all this was that "midpoint in time" when Jesus was here on earth. It is flanked by some references to Israel's history (in Luke 1–2 and elsewhere) and the ongoing history of the people of God after Pentecost. The pioneering work on this theological outline of history was developed especially by Hans Conzelmann, and while the validity of some of its details has been debated, much of Conzelmann's analysis has become standard fare, as in the sketch of Lukan theology by Joseph A. Fitzmyer.[20] Certain of its features are worthy of special attention, such as the contention that Luke treats Israel in a way that commends the piety of Elizabeth and Zechariah, Anna and Simeon, but no longer regards the law as a problem; and the manner in which the life of Jesus is presented as the "midpoint of time," to use Conzelmann's phrase, when "the Dayspring from on high visited us" and pardon and mercy were extended as never before. It was the year of "jubilee" (4:18-19, 21; cf. Isa. 61:1-2; Lev. 23).

This Lukan theology of historical eras is, as noted above, also geographical — a tale of two cities, as it were — Jerusalem and Rome. It takes the position that Jerusalem was the geographical center of the universe and that it remained dominant in the life of the church. When one combines this with the Old Testament idea that "out of Zion the word goes forth" (Isa. 2:3; Ps. 50:2; cf. Ps. 53:6), then it is possible to speak of a theological program: from God's city the gospel now moves forth into the world and grows.

Luke also achieves in his telling of the story of Jesus and Christian origins a further goal: he describes how to live in the world of Caesar, in Roman cities, within "pagan" society, amid Greek culture. Has Luke-Acts sold out to bourgeois society? Not if one takes seriously the date (about A.D. 90) and situation in which this evangelist-historian worked. For he has shown how Christians could be at home in the world of the Roman Empire while anchored in the Christ event and without letting go of the hope that Christ would come again.

This last trend can also be illustrated through the Pastoral Epistles. (Some, in fact, now suggest that 1 and 2 Timothy and

Titus are also the work of St. Luke, a "third volume" as it were, to round out Luke-Acts.)[21] These letters, which present guidelines for the church and its leaders, show how the Christian community can settle down for the long haul in history. The parousia hope is retained, but it seems a good deal more distant. In the growing decades of Christian existence, patterns appear for church structure, social relations, the orthodox faith, and piety. With such ingredients, including doctrine, ministry, and organizational structure, the stage is set for Christians to reflect more fully on history and tell of its meaning from the standpoint of the coming of Jesus Christ.

Several aspects of Lukan theology are important for our understanding of salvation history and stewardship.

(1) Luke stresses the sequence "Jesus Christ, then the Spirit." While he presents the Spirit as active throughout all three eras — Israel, Jesus, and the church — Luke-Acts, as no other New Testament writing, presents a "shift of the eons" after Easter and at Pentecost through the ascension and the dramatic outpouring of the Spirit by the ascended Lord. In this way Luke suggests a *new era,* in which Jesus is absent and the Spirit is the means for the presence of God.

(2) Luke comes to terms with the Roman political world and Greek culture. Convinced as he is that Christ will tarry before returning, Luke is anxious to help Christians live in a world that previously had seemed alien and hostile. Luke is *world-affirming* in a way that Paul and John were not. He embraces good Greek, cites pagan poets, praises Roman justice, and in some ways presents an *apologia* for Christianity to the Empire. Because of certain of these features and the way he chose to represent Paul (some would say *mis*represent Paul), Luke has sometimes been seen as a forerunner of "early Catholicism" and an enemy of true Christianity in the third generation. Like it or not, however, we find in his writings pointers for Christians on how to come to terms with worldly power and not remain, sociologically, a sect of outsiders.

(3) A particular form of this coming to terms with power and responsibility occurs in Luke's treatment of *wealth and poverty*. It is well known that he emphasizes stewardship of wealth, the blessedness of the (economically) poor, and the right use of resources. While his exact emphases continue to be debated — it has been variously argued that Luke is a theologian of revolution (on the basis of Luke 1:51-53), that it is his intent to show how the rich too can be saved (Luke 19:1-10, the basis for a later treatise on the topic by Clement of Alexandria),[22] or that he stresses almsgiving[23] — it is at least clear that Luke combines heilsgeschichte and stewardship. His two volumes have been used as a basis for many of the insights of liberation theology as well as for arguments that one can be well-to-do and still be responsibly Christian.

b. *Paul* provides a second example. It has been hotly contested whether there is heilsgeschichte in his theology or not. Those who deplore Luke's theology of salvation history are disinclined to see it in Paul's letters. Others, such as Johannes Munck and Krister Stendahl, make it central for interpreting Paul.[24]

To plunge into the issues, the view of history expressed in the writings of Paul the apostle — some would even say his "philosophy of history" — is marked by at least two themes.[25]

One is the pervasiveness of sin. In kinship with the Yahwist or J writer in Genesis 3 (the story of "the fall") and the outlook now documented in the Dead Sea Scrolls from the Qumran community, there is in the Pauline writings a suggestion that humanity is in bondage and cannot do the good it wills before God. All persons, Jew and Gentile alike, have sinned and keep falling short of the glory God intends for them (Rom. 3:23). They lack the image of God, which now only the Lord Jesus Christ possesses (Rom. 1:23; 8:28; Col. 1:15; 3:10; 2 Cor. 3:18; 1 Cor. 15:49). So it is that people are "locked up" under Sin (Gal. 3:22), above all in bondage to what Herbert Butterfield termed the capital sin that "locks people up in all their other sins, and fastens men and nations more tightly than ever in all their other predicaments . . . namely the sin of self-righteousness"; this root sin multiplies "all the tragedies of the centuries" and "brings us to . . . that messianic hoax," the pretense that we've just about got it made: "just one little war more against the last remaining enemies of righteousness, and then the world will be cleansed, and we can start building Paradise."[26] Only God's saving righteousness can correct and achieve that.

Second, Paul accepted the view growing up in the Judaism of his day concerning "two ages." This was the apocalyptic belief that there is, on the one hand, "the present evil age," under the dominion of Satan (Gal. 1:4), and on the other hand "the age to come." Paul came to associate the age to come with the new creaturehood into which one enters by baptism in the name of Jesus (2 Cor. 5:17; Gal. 3:27-28). Paul believed that Christians begin to be part of God's new age, though they have not yet fully arrived. There is always, for Paul, a future fulfillment, which will occur at the parousia, when Christ comes at the end.

So it is that Paul's thought focuses on Jesus' cross and resurrection as the central event of history and yet also ranges all the way from creation to the end of the world or of the ages. We can get at Paul's view of this total history in any of a number of ways that have been treated in detail by experts in Pauline theology (and, assuredly, debated vigorously too).

One method is to look at the seminal figures in God's plan and work of salvation, as we can identify them and their functions from Paul's letters.[27] The focus falls on five major figures in the story of humanity: Adam, Abraham, Moses, Christ, and the Second Adam.

The first (or earthly) Adam was the figure in Paul's thought whose disobedience put all of humankind under the dominion of Sin and death. See especially Rom. 5:12-21 and 1 Cor. 15:21-22.

Abraham was the representative figure, for Jew and Gentile alike, who showed what faith in God's promise means, a promise fulfilled in his "seed" or descendant, Jesus Christ (Gal. 3; Rom. 4).

Moses seems in Paul's letters an otiose figure. He is associated with the giving of the Law at Sinai, an expression of God's will, to be sure, but an expression that never brought salvation. He is seen in light of Christ, in contrast to Christ, and also in contrast to Abraham (Gal. 3:17-24; 1 Cor. 10:1-12; 2 Cor. 3, reflecting Exod. 34:29-35).

Jesus Christ, a son of David (Rom. 1:3), relates to all these prior figures as the One to Come, the Second Adam who brings life (1 Cor. 15:45). Christ is the Abrahamic seed in whom the promise is fulfilled (Gal. 3:16), the great contrast to Moses, and above all the exalted Lord, working in both redemption and creation.

Christ is also the the the last Adam, the One to come in the future (Rom. 5:14). There is "eschatological history now in progress" and a fulfillment in the future after this time of "eschatological flux."[28] The "new creation" applies to the individual believer (via justification), to the church, and ultimately also to the world.

The historical schema of Pauline theology have also been spelled out in other ways, even more elaborately; graphical representations of these alternative constructions are available in several presentations of the apostle's theology.[29]

A second way to comprehend Paul's view of history is to take up his hope for Israel. The paradigm passage is, of course, Romans 9–11. The schema here can be said to begin with the present situation, *in medias res:* Paul the Jew preaches Christ, but his "kindred by race" to a considerable extent reject Jesus. One can also see at work Paul's historical reading of the past, in the history of election. This runs from Abraham's time on (9:6-33). Paul's bold hope for the future is that, after this period during which "a hardening has come upon part of Israel," the "full number of the Gentiles [will] come in, and so all Israel will be saved" (11:25-26). Few sections of the Bible are written with greater personal pathos (cf. 9:3). Scholars who have made these chapters the heart of Pauline thought often find here a missionary view of history that involves three phases: (1) rejection of the gospel by Israel, (2) acceptance of it by the Gentiles, and (3) eventual salvation for Israel. Further treatments of this material are provided by Munck and those influenced by his view of salvation history such as Krister Stendahl.[30]

A third approach involves detailed attention to the collection project that Paul launched in his Gentile churches for "the saints at Jerusalem." This was not simply a fund for the poor or an early kind of Church World Service, built around "One Great Hour of Sharing," a sort of caritative act. Nor was it only an ecumenical project to bring together two wings of the church, uniting his Gentile congregations with the mother church of Jewish Christianity, though it was that. Rather, the collection can be seen as a part of God's plan. Here we can speak of a consciousness on the part of Paul and some of his converts that they were "makers of eschatological history" or at least an important part in God's plan by participating in an offering that would climax all history. For Paul's plan seems to have been that he and delegates from the congregations would bring the money to Jerusalem and then he would go on to Rome and from there to Spain for the cherished mission venture in Hispania. Surely history would then draw to its close, the gospel having been preached in a representative way to all the world (Rom. 11:25-26; 15:19, 23-29); Christ would come, and God would be all in all.

The considerable number of texts about the collection in Paul's letters (1 Cor. 16:1-4; 2 Cor. 8–9; Rom. 15:25-31; cf. Gal. 2:10, as well as Acts 20:24 and 24:17) and the significant secondary literature on the topic[31] deserve more attention than they have typically received in stewardship discussions. In particular, attention ought to be paid to what are likely two separate letters by Paul now embedded in 2 Corinthians, the one addressed to Corinth (chap. 8), the other to Christians in the surrounding province of Achaia (chap. 9), but both about "the offering for the saints."

In these latter passages Hans Dieter Betz has called attention to what can best be termed an aberrant line of theology that Paul employs in appealing for support for the collection, a line of argument that has clear parallels in Greek sources.[32] Paul seems to argue that God's grace will cause bountiful giving, and this in turn will lead to many more thanksgivings to God, because of these gifts. There is, further, an argument from agriculture in 2 Corinthians 9:8-12, about how God's bounty leads to further blessings.[33] An appeal to the Greek virtue of equality follows: while the churches in Greece were at the time supporting the Jewish Christians in Palestine, there might come a time when Jewish Christians would reciprocate and supply the wants of those in Greece (8:13-15).[34] Some subsequent fund-raisers have reveled in these arguments! One wonders if Paul incorporated them from the Greek world of the day on his own or derived them from his converts in Macedonia or even picked them up from the Jerusalem Christians for whom he was seeking support.

We do not know the outcome of Paul's collection appeal, for all his references to it appear in letters written during the time when the funds were still being gathered. Not even Acts tells us of the outcome; indeed, Acts is virtually silent about the project itself. Many think the collection was not accepted by the Jewish Christians in Jerusalem.[35] In any case, according to the Acts account, Paul was arrested in Jerusalem and was sent as a prisoner to Rome, where he likely suffered martyrdom and was thus prevented from undertaking the mission to Spain with which he hoped to culminate his career. But the collection project suggests how he thought of his work in the church and in and for the world — eschatologically and as part of God's plan for salvation history. It included money to aid other Christians.

Perhaps there is also a fourth way to get at Paul's thinking with regard to God's work in history and his own role in it and the place of other Christians. It has to do with his use of vocabulary from the root word *oikonomia* against the background of the varied classical meanings sketched in Chapter I above.

Paul clearly thought of himself and other Christians as "servants of Christ and stewards [*oikonomoi*] of the mysteries of God" (1 Cor. 4:1). The Church Fathers incorrectly saw in this use of the term "mysteries" a reference to the sacraments; in fact, however, Paul was using the Greek word here against a Semitic background in order to refer to God's revealed secrets, open secrets now made known, which are part of the divine plan.[36] There is a background here in apocalyptic passages such as Daniel 2:19, 28, 29, and so forth. Paul understood that God had a plan of salvation that was being worked out in human history, through Christ. Of this *oikonomia* —for that is the term Paul employs — he was himself a minister, to proclaim what God had done (see Col. 1:25; 1 Cor. 9:17; Eph. 1:10; 3:2). The apostle thus saw a role for himself in the economy of God. Indeed, 1 Peter 4:10 indicates that all Christians have such roles as "good stewards of the manifold grace of God," serving others with "whatever gift each of you has received" (NRSV).

From this small passage about stewardship and God's *oikonomia* grew the vocabulary developed by the Church Fathers into the grand argument for an economy or plan or rule of God in history, in which church and individuals all play a role.

There are other passages in the New Testament that might be used to support a view of heilsgeschichte, notably in Matthew's Gospel and the Epistle to the Hebrews. But in whatever form we choose to cast it, heilsgeschichte, as the story of salvation worked by God, is at the heart of any Christian concept of stewardship. For centuries some version or other of the economy of God was central, and much of the best in North American stewardship has been a response to it or, better put, has seen itself as part of the ongoing story of redemption and service. It is a factor without which we ought not to speak of *Christian* stewardship at all.

B. Stewardship, Creation, and the Role of All Humanity within the Economy of God

Stewardship in North America began as fund-raising for domestic ministries and Christian mission in the world. At its heart, down through the 1960s, at least, has been the story of salvation. People say, "I respond because of God's gifts to me," or "I give because of what Christ has done for me." In scriptural terms, "We love because God first loved us" (1 John 4:19); "Freely ye have received, freely give" (Matt. 10:8, KJV).

But our understanding of what the theme of stewardship takes in has changed immensely in the last decade or so. The interests and expectations of leaders in stewardship, such as those attending conferences sponsored by the NCCUSA Commission on Stewardship, whether church staff people or theological essayists, have shifted since the sixties. The lectures and books of Douglas John Hall are emblematic of and partly responsible for this shift, if not typical for the outlook of all those who are involved in the stewardship work of U.S. and Canadian churches. As we have seen, Hall contends that the "new stewardship" endorses the principles of globalization, communalization, ecologization, politicization, and futurization.

But these principles of the new stewardship are by no means unique to Christians. Global concern, communalism, ecological awareness, political action, and futurism — whatever these things mean — are common coin for Jews, Buddhists, Marxists, and atheists as well. There is nothing per se religious, let alone Christian, about any of them. If one were to seek support for such an approach from Romans 8:22 — "the whole creation has been groaning in travail together until now" — one would have to have to add that it was groaning in travail because of smog, acid rain, pesticides in the food chain, and depletion of the ozone layer.

If such are the issues to be addressed under the aegis of stewardship, it is necessary to ask whether the Christian understanding outlined above under heilsgeschichte suffices. Or must we now speak of several types of stewardship, only one of which is based on salvation history?

1. Stewardship — Christian, Theistic, or Atheistic?

Christian stewardship is understandable. Followers of Jesus invented it. Believers do things in life because, as Paul put it, the love of God exhibited in Jesus Christ and our love toward Christ impel us to do these things for others (2 Cor. 5:14).

But is there not also a stewardship practiced, at least in some matters, by people who do *not* believe in Jesus Christ? Cannot a Jew be moved by the God of Israel and by the law of Moses, to tithe, to be concerned about the land (not just of Israel or wherever Jews live but the whole earth), and to be involved for justice and peace? Jewish "freedom riders" joined in the civil rights struggle in the United States alongside Protestants and Catholics. And what about other world religions? Consider the traditional love for the earth of people indigenous to North America, for instance.[37] Whatever the name by which God is called, there can be, under God, a passion for ecology, political equality, and many other principles that have recently been gathered under the umbrella of stewardship. We might refer to this as "theistic stewardship" — that is to say, a concept of people as stewards motivated by a God other than "the Father of our Lord Jesus Christ."

It is perhaps more difficult to conceive of an atheistic stewardship. Such a stewardship obviously could not be based on Christ's work for human beings or even an understanding of the world as the gift of a beneficent God. But why not a simple utilitarian concern for pure water or an unpolluted atmosphere as requisite for human happiness and well-being? Or for the sake of children not yet born (the Marxist eschatology of generations to come)? We can scarcely suppose that concern about the dying of the Aral Sea is restricted solely to those of Russian Orthodox or Jewish heritage. Unbelievers have their reasons to care as well. So it does make sense to speak of "atheistic stewardship."

Indeed, we have to take account of "stewardship" terms outside a narrowly Christian context, since there has been an amazing comeback and multiplication of usages during the past decade. It was not too long ago that books on stewardship themes skirted the term or dropped it entirely. "Secular" usage of the term had dwindled to such examples as airline stewardesses and

97

union shop stewards. Only a few, such as Wallace Fisher, fought a rearguard action to keep the term "stewardship" alive.[38]

Now, to our amazement, the term is everywhere. The term is used widely in the popular press to connote efficient management, as in the criticism that a NASA official was "often autocratic in his stewardship of the astronaut corps." Another example involves a racetrack owner in Tijuana, Mexico, who was known as "the Abominable Snowman" because of "the wide perception that he has a fondness for cocaine"; the New York *Times* spoke critically of the man's "stewardship of the race track and other family businesses." Does this usage approach the "shady" sense of *oikonomia* sometimes found in classical usage,[39] or does it imply an expected ethic from which the man fell short?

2. The Growth of "Creation Motifs" in Stewardship

For some who have been involved in recent stewardship work, it is probably unnecessary to spell out how, in recent literature, stewardship has been extended to take in what might be called the "creation motif." This is especially evident in the new concern for the earth that has arisen in a variety of contexts, from a farm crisis brought on by low prices and drought to the acid rain menace, which poses a threat in Ontario and in northeast U.S. states and at the little natural lake near Hamlin, Pennsylvania, where much of this book was drafted and revised.

The impetus for such thinking has always been present in the Bible, as we shall see. A famous address by the Chicago theologian Joseph Sittler, published in his book *The Care of the Earth,* was an early expression on the theme.[40] One should take good care of the lake simply because it's there and because we can enjoy it more if it's free from pollution. And of course we have already noted Douglas John Hall's resounding endorsement of ecology as a part of stewardship.

But we have to ask what sort of theological base for stewardship we can turn to if heilsgeschichte will not do. As a practical matter, how do we appeal to all those who do not name the name of Jesus Christ to join with believers in such matters? It will scarcely do to suggest that they are operating on the basis of a secret christology or assume that we have resolved the problem by characterizing them as "anonymous Christians." Such proposals are ultimately demeaning to the personhood of non-Christians. So how can we openly address and advocate stewardship in a pluralistic context? A biblical basis, particularly as developed by the Church Fathers out of views prevalent in the Greco-Roman world, may prove helpful.

3. A Biblical-Hellenistic Basis

Let us return to the theme of "the economy of God," particularly as developed among Stoics and others in the Hellenistic world.

a. *The Greco-Roman Background.* E. P. Hatch can serve us as a guide to how the Greek ideas and practices, as he calls them, came into prominence in the patristic church.[41]

As we have already noted, the idea of a divine administration of the universe was widespread in the Mediterranean world and beyond in the pre-Christian era. This rule and management of all things was described variously as the *oikonomia* of Zeus, Providence, Nature, Fate, Destiny, or Reason and as the divine *dioikēsis.* The latter is a word related to *oikonomia.* From it is derived the term "diocese," which, in an ecclesiastical context, refers to a region in which a bishop has authority; in a secular context, it was once used to refer to an administrative subdivision in the Roman Empire.

This Hellenistic "administration of God" in the heavens and throughout the world was not based, as in Israel's thought, on the experience of Yahweh's having become king by a battle victory in history (cf. Exod. 15; Pss. 97–99), nor did Greek thought always attribute the kingship of Zeus to a mythical victory in a battle at creation, as in Mesopotamian myth.[42] Rather, the Greeks maintained that by observing the order of nature one could reason to an orderly creator and ruler of all things who controls the universe. The author of this pervasive order and unity was God, whether called, in various religions, Zeus, Osiris, Baal, or by people of reason "the Logos," or simply "the divine." A number of terms were applied to this ruling deity in antiquity, including *ho dioikētēs* and *ho dioikōn* or *oikonomōn,* "the administrator" or "the one who manages or administers" all things.

We do well to recall that the Greek word for the world, *kosmos,* means basically "order," and could also be used as a term for God. The creator and the creation were not distinguished, as in biblical thought, but were fused, so that God became a sort of "world soul," as in pantheism (and in some forms of modern process theology). Colossians 1:18 is a Christian protest against such thinking, for it designates as the "body" of the deity, in this case Christ, not the world but the church.[43]

In any case, much of Greek philosophy, particularly on the popular level, was marked by the claim that the world is under God's management or economy, an *oikonomia* concerned with management of things in the present and not just with ancient origins at a beginning of creation.

Hatch calls attention to three aspects of the Greek view of God that proved fruitful for Jewish and then Christian use,[44] and a fourth can be added. First comes the notion of *one Supreme Being.* "One God" is a slogan to which not only Deuteronomy 6:4 and 1 Corinthians 8:6 could resonate but also at least a portion of the pagan world. Second, this one God rules as *creator* of this world. The human observer was expected to reason from order in nature to an orderly creator. Irenaeus, as a Christian thinker, was later able to say that the "Rule of Truth" includes the concept of "one Almighty God . . . creating all things, disposing, and governing all things," but then he added in specifically Christian terms, "through his Word and Spirit."[45] Hatch's third point is that this deity is a *moral governor* who incorporates both justice and goodness into the divine reign. There is benevolence in the deity's administration over all.

To this outline a fourth point may be appended: *human beings* could play *a role* in the divine administration of the universe. Dio Chrysostom in his *Orations* before the Emperor Trajan, circa A.D. 98, urged the new ruler to imitate the way Zeus administers the universe.[46] On a much more everyday level, Epictetus, the former slave from Hierapolis turned philosopher, called on everyone to study the divine *dioikēsis* of the universe in order to "find your place in God's dispensation" and live as a "citizen [not of Athens but] of the world" and a child of God.[47] Quoting Cleanthes, he rhapsodized, "Lead thou me on, O Zeus, and thou too, O Destiny."[48]

Such Stoicism was congenial to rapprochement with Judaism and development in Christianity, as Hatch suggested. So-called "pagan" writers (some urge that the term no longer be used, on the grounds that it is pejorative), non-Jewish and pre-Christian philosophers, thus set forth a basis of appeal for people to observe and analyze the world, to be concerned about its well-being as God's creation, and to act for the common welfare.

b. *Some Examples in Biblical Theology.* The scriptural bases for a "theology of creation" are better known and require less elaboration.

The New Testament suggests clearly how such faith statements about God and the Christ of God grew up. No one would have dreamed of making statements during Jesus' lifetime or even immediately after the first Easter Day connecting the prophet-teacher from Nazareth with the creation of the world. Jesus himself spoke rather about *God's* beneficent care of human beings, birds and beasts, and the lilies of the field (Matt. 6:25-33). The earliest Christian preaching was about the lordship of the risen Jesus, that he would return in glory, and how indeed, as Christ, Jesus now reigns at God's right hand. But by A.D. 50 or 60 Christians were confessing Jesus also as God's vicegerent at the creation of the world (1 Cor. 8:6; Col. 1:15-20) and the agent for God in providentially holding the world together (Heb. 1:2-3a). As these examples suggest, belief in Jesus Christ with regard to creation grew out of faith in Jesus as present lord and returning judge. Faith wished to project back to the beginning what it experienced in the present and hoped for in the future.[49]

In the Hebrew Scriptures the course of development must have been similar. It is not that Israel first believed in the creation story of Genesis 1 (for that Priestly account is actually one of the last parts of the Hebrew Bible to have been written down) and only then came to "exodus faith" in Yahweh as Redeemer. No, at the heart of Israel's experience was the deliverance from Egypt. But in time, and at certain points in Israel's long history, "creation faith" arose and indeed proved most necessary. There were occasions when faith in God as initial and continuing Creator took on an importance and independence of its own, as has been true at times for Christianity.[50]

For Israel one of those moments came when Isaiah of Babylon invoked creation to rally the exiled remnant of the faithful to the hope of a return to Zion; these poetic lines are preserved in Isaiah 40–55. When this prophet lived, it is likely that the redemptive tidings of the exodus no longer carried the force they once did and, moreover, by the waters of Babylon the children of Israel were surrounded by creation motifs about Marduk, the Babylonian deity. And so the prophet made what Yahweh did at creation, intertwined with echoes of the release from Egyptian bondage, the basis of appeal (Isa. 44:24-27; 51:9-11).[51] Something of the same sort can be said of the Priestly writer, who anchored the Priestly saga in creation, with such details as the claim that God set the sun and moon in the firmament of heaven precisely in order to provide astral regulation for the Sabbath, the monthly, and the annual liturgical festivals commanded in the Law (Gen. 1:14-16).[52] Psalm 104 is a hymn to God the Creator employing lines out of ancient Near Eastern thought and specifically the Egyptian "Hymn to the Aton" or Sun-God.[53] These lines are now used to praise Yahweh, including the thought from the Egyptian version that people "live (only) through thee," O Aton (cf. Ps. 104:27-30).

For the New Testament a similar linkage with knowledge of God in the Gentile world is made several times. This claim has to do especially with knowledge of God's power and deity and even beneficence (see, e.g., Rom. 1:20-21). The link can be used in a negative, critical way, to show people their shortcomings and failure to achieve the glory and image of God that the Lord expects (Rom. 1; 3:23). The motif can also be employed more positively, as an opening for preaching Jesus and the resurrection, as in Paul's address at the Areopagus (Acts 17:16-31).

The overall conclusion is by now apparent. Whether in Greek and Roman thought (and in other religions too) or in biblical testimony, one can speak of an appeal to creation, the Creator, providence, and ongoing divine care for the world and can use this to motivate people to respond as good stewards. Not everything need be based on heilsgeschichte. Christians, of course, rest on both types of theology. But you don't have to believe in Jesus Christ or the God of Israel to share in the creational approach. All persons can. Some, indeed, like people indigenous to North America, find it quite natural.

Two types of stewardship therefore emerge: one based on faith in Christ as well as in divine creation, and the other based solely on the world as a divine gift or place to exercise stewardship. Both reflect a divine economy. Here is a pillar, in the economy of creation, on which to base appeals that require action by people other than Christians. That covers a great deal of and in the world.

C. Stewardship and the Future: The Place of the Apocalyptic Outlook in the Economy of God

There may also be a third approach to stewardship, from the angle of the future of God and the world. It is a motif that in the Bible and Christian life is often expressed in apocalyptic terms. But is this avenue of thought worth taking up? Some argue that all such apocalyptic, futurist thinking and writing, even in Scripture, actually poses a threat to the stewardship venture.

1. "Apocalyptic" a Menace to Stewardship?

One such critic of apocalyptic thinking is Douglas John Hall. He seems to claim that, if stewardship now "means that we are responsible for the globe" together, in a "stewardship of many creatures" (including "the nonhuman"), and if we are called to employ a "theology of nature" for the care of the world so that God's will might "be done *on earth*," then we must "set our faces against those who write off the earth and look for heavenly solace to earthly grief."[54] More sharply, he states that "apocalyptic sectarianism is the visible tip of an ecclesiastical iceberg."[55] Elsewhere, Hall writes that the world is torn between "an ecumenical (catholic) sense of the world" and "imperial striving that may end in Armageddon," though it is never clear whether he wishes to blame Christianity's failure to hold (his view of) a proper stewardship on the "imperial establishment" of Constantine and subsequent rulers or on the "apocalyptic viewpoint" that spiritualized the notion of the world, or on both.[56]

But if we are to turn away from apocalyptic thought, it is not clear how much of the New Testament will remain acceptable. Indeed, Hall speculates that some of these unfortunate dimensions of Christian teaching "are from Jesus himself" and became dominant because of the fact that "in the contents of that very apocalyptic age many people had already given up on the world."[57] Presumably that includes Paul also. Exclude his epistles, many of Jesus' teachings, and, of course, the book of Revelation and Mark 13, the "little apocalypse," and one is left with very little from the New Testament canon. Chiefly Luke-Acts! That is to offer a very selective reading of history and Scripture. One must be careful, in the desire to flay modern sectarians, not to throw out the baby with the bathwater. Hall offers a more careful discussion of this material in *Imaging God* (pp. 26-42); here the classical Christian ambiguity about this world is well observed, though Hall wishes to transcend all this in favor of a "conversion *to* the world" (italics added).

Theodore S. Horvath has pressed the same sort of argument even more poignantly and bluntly, contending that there are two threats to history as we move into "a new era in our understanding of stewardship" — nuclear holocaust and millennial expectations. Threats of a nuclear holocaust violate the peacemaking impulse of stewardship, he says, and millennial expectations of the rapture and so forth are intrinsically "world-negating," "anti-history," and "anti-stewardship."[58]

These are weighty charges, and very easy for people to take up and run with, since in seeking identity churches often seem to need some other group *against which* to define themselves or, in the vernacular, to "beat up on." It has become unfashionable for Protestants, at least in the mainline denominations, to find their object for counter-identity in Catholics and Jews, and so the *bête noire* for many Protestants has become "the Fundamentalists" or in particular wild-eyed sect groups of Armageddon persuasion. Such a stance, of course, is simply to return the compliment regarding how such groups think about liberal Protestantism or mainline Christianity, which, in their opinion, has become void of "real Christian faith," if not apostate.

Before going further with such charges against sectarians, it is important to try to understand something about the apocalyptic outlook and its possible values for us. For this approach to God's actions and goal is curiously intertwined with the divine *oikonomia* too.

2. The Origin and Characteristics of Apocalyptic Eschatology

Over the years there has grown up in biblical studies a widely shared view of apocalypticism as a particular type of eschatology. It is said to have originated in Persian Zoroastrianism and to have stressed from the outset a cosmic dualism, the notion that two forces contend for mastery throughout the universe. According to Martin Rist in 1962, the apocalyptic pattern of expression is usually marked by visions of the future, a pseudonymous author, sometimes the expectation of a messiah figure, elaborate angelology and ranks of demons (the cosmic dualism personified), symbolism involving animals and sometimes numbers, astral features (e.g., a heavenly Jerusalem), and woes and troubles soon to come.[59]

More recent research, however, both into a growing number of ancient documents that reflect the apocalyptic mind-set and sociologically into the nature of apocalyptic groups today and in the past, has led to a rethinking of the topic.[60] Scholars now distinguish between *apocalypticism* as a system of thought, *apocalypse* as a literary genre used to transmit thinking of this type, and *apocalyptic eschatology* as "a way of viewing divine plans in relation to mundane realities."[61]

More precisely, apocalyptic eschatology views "the future as the context of divine saving and judging activity . . . as a continuation of prophetic eschatology." Indeed, it was not simply a "Persian transplant" but developed along the lines of classical Israelite prophetism and was influenced by other sources, including wisdom literature and Greek/Hellenistic ideas.[62] Apocalyptic eschatology differs from prophetic eschatology, which sought to integrate human activity into the divine will and plan, in the extent to which it "lets God be God" and sees solutions not in political structures of human connivance but only in "a new transformed order" that Yahweh will bring about (Isa. 65:17, "behold, I create new heavens and a new earth").

Under what circumstances does such apocalypticism arise, introducing its own "symbolic universe" of values that are often at odds with the prevailing culture and societal structures? According to Hanson, "all ancient apocalyptic movements are characterized by (a) a particular type of social setting, and (b) a related group response."[63] The social setting, in a word, is alienation — specifically, the alienation of some group from the socio-religious myths of the larger culture. Members of this group are characteristically "disenfranchised from institutional structures and reduced to powerlessness." They view their world as disintegrating, and in response they develop their own worldview from an alternative perspective. They hammer out an identity in contradistinction to the rest of the world and develop a vision of ultimate vindication for their own values. There is thus a denial of the world's structures based on "a vision of what God is doing on a cosmic level to effect deliverance and salvation."[64] Hanson suggests that there are two basic types of apocalyptic movements, one of "marginal persons within a nation who feel alienated from the symbol system of the dominant society," the other of "a broad cross section of a nation protesting against a symbolic universe which has been imposed on them by a foreign power."[65]

Such groups appeared in Israel's history from the sixth century B.C. on, and also in the early Christian era. The book of Revelation, for example, shows "how apocalyptic forms and images were transformed in the early church" to show how "the sovereign God was very much in control of history" and how Christians reflected a "nonviolent political posture" in the face of persecution.[66]

Insights like these have reshaped our understanding of the apocalyptic outlook and therefore our evaluation of it. Such analysis is applicable not only to the early Maccabean movement, hasidic Judaism, and much of early Christianity in the Roman Empire (prior to Luke-Acts) but also to a considerable degree persons of color in the United States and Canada today, the underclasses in most Latin American countries, and many Christians behind the Iron Curtain prior to *perestroika* and *glasnost*. If, as Hall contends, there has always been a "thin line" of the "disenfranchised" running through Christianity,[67] one suspects that they have often been apocalyptists. Even if such groups represent one-sided outbursts against the dominant culture, they might well be able to provide vital insights to the mainline churches. It is important that we consider the pros and cons of apocalypticism.

3. *The Value of a Futurist Approach*

On the negative side, there is always a danger in apocalyptic approaches of *abandoning this earth*. As Hall rightly emphasizes, apocalyptists may retreat into political quietism. This is not to say that they are the only sorts of Christians to do so, however; this impulse is evident among pietists, monastics, and those in the Anabaptist tradition, too, for example. Nor is it to say that the opposite extreme is not also problematic — caesaropapism and the like. The point is simply that apocalypticism is by nature world-negating, and this can lead to passivity. It threatens to remove God from this present world, except as judge. But we must remember the reason: the group perceives the imposed culture and its struc-tures to be so bankrupt that no compromise or reform is possible.

From this stance there often follows another characteristic that must be criticized: a certain *arrogance*, even toward those who confess the same savior and toward other churches, an arrogance stemming in part from the group's certainty about what God has planned for the next few years or weeks, right down to the last detail. This breeds an in-group, us-versus-them mentality that only exacerbates the picture others have of the apocalyptic group and leads the group to dig in defensively all the more. If the group's "predictions" do not pan out, the members will usu-ally find ways to reinterpret either the events or their guiding oracles and move on to new visions of the future.

On the positive side, however, are a number of factors.

1. Apocalyptic thought is typically oriented to *the future* rather than to the past or to the present. Apocalyptic groups have a shining vision of what is to be. Evidences of such vision can be found in Jewish messianism, apocalyptic Christianity, most views of evolution, and the secular eschatology of Marxism.

2. Apocalyptic groups typically teach that *the kingdoms of this world* should *not* be identified with *the kingdom of God*. "Not by might, nor by power, but by my Spirit, says the LORD of hosts" (Zech. 4:6).

3. Apocalyptic thought characteristically *protests* all notions of *natural evolution,* assertions that humanity is progressing toward the new Jerusalem on earth, building the kingdom, or every day in every way getting better and better. This point can cut in several ways, against liberal Protestantism as well as the pretensions of an individual nation (like the United States) to promote itself as "the promised land" or expected Zion.

4. Apocalyptists see clearly that the kingdom, the power, the glory, and the victory are *God's, not ours.* It is Yahweh, or the Lord's Christ, who will bring the vision of peace to pass, not we ourselves.[68] It may be that in certain situations apocalyptic categories offer the only means by which to state that salvation is God's doing or to defend the emphasis on "Christ alone" *(solus Christus)* or the other *sola* formulations of the Reformation. It is no accident that the book of Relevation had immense importance in the Nazi period and Second World War or that church windows in German churches of the 1950s often used motifs from that book.

5. There is a final emphasis that is dependent in part, but not fully, on the apocalyptic outlook. It is what in studies of Paul's thought is sometimes called the apostle's *"future reservation."* For all Paul says about the work of Christ being fully accomplished and about the gift of justification or of life in Christ being present among us already, he never pretends that believers "have it all," totally and completely, in this life. There is a reservation about the fullness of salvation now, for there is an aspect still to come, which is often expressed in apocalyptic terms. In Cullmann's phraseology, the believers are "no longer" what they once were, but they are "not yet" what they will be.[69]

This future emphasis has implications not only for our understanding of Christian identity but also for the manner in which Christians should live, something ethicists have called the "as if" principle. The concept and the phrase itself can be found in 1 Corinthians 7:29-31, a passage with an apocalyptic setting, for Paul notes that this world (or age) is passing away, and "the time is very short." Therefore Christians are to live "as if" (NRSV "as though")[70] they are not dependent on the world or its relationships. All ties of business and even family and marriage are penultimate, not ultimate, and even in our deepest commitments to people and things of this world there ought to be a detachment that keeps us from substituting them for God.

Stewardship involves distinguishing penultimate relationships, to say nothing of antepenultimate relationships, from the ultimate relationship with the one true God. Making such distinctions frees the Christian, making possible a critical distance from the world.[71] This is what enables one to make judgments on the "reification of existing institutions,"[72] to "mourn as though not mourning," and to "rejoice as though not rejoicing" (7:30). The climactic word appears in 1 Corinthians 7:32: "I want you to be free from anxieties" — in order, of course, better to serve, as good stewards. In keeping with this, Christians "neither condemn nor idolize the world," says Wolfgang Schrage; "they neither flee it nor embrace it."[73] It is by no means easy to maintain such a dialectical view, but it would seem to be prescribed by a New Testament eschatology that is at times apocalyptically expressed.

A hermeneutic for approaching the apocalyptic outlook, in a time when there is a "recrudescence of apocalypticism," is needed in many ways. Paul Hanson's discussions of the phenomenon have begun to sketch just such an approach.[74]

There is a final skeleton in the closet of stewardship and themes related to the Greek word *oikonomia*. In some ways it relates also to apocalyptic schemes concerning the history of the world and God's plan for the end. It has to do with an aspect of apocalypticism best described as "periods" or stages in salvation history.

4. "Eras" or Periodization in God's Plan

In their broad surveys of world events, apocalyptic writers frequently divide history up into a series of ages or periods. They view the divine plan as unfolding in a sequence of eras. At a minimum they distinguish between "this age" and "the age to come," as we have noted. The former is often said to be under Satan's domination; in the latter, Yahweh will act and reign. Some apocalyptic schemes involve a series of kingdoms. Daniel 7, for instance, speaks of four kingdoms, each of which is symbolized by a beast figure — a lion, a bear, a leopard, and a dragon-like creature — until at last, in contrast to all of these, a human figure appears, representing the battered remnant of Israel's faithful. In a more elaborate example, the prediction in Jeremiah 25:11-12 that Israel's exile would last seventy years before God intervened to restore the remnant and punish Babylon was reworked in Daniel 9 as "seventy weeks of years" (i.e., 490 years), a period lasting to the days of the Maccabees. An apocalyptic section in the book of Enoch predicts "a week" between the two ages. Actually the passages in Enoch 91:12-17 and 93:1-10 present events that are to happen during a period of three plus seven (for a total of ten) weeks, followed by "many weeks without number forever" when "sin shall no more be heard of forever."[75]

The New Testament reflects only in a modest way such a worldview, but it does appear in both Jesus' teaching (Mark 10:30) and Paul's letters (Gal. 1:4), not to mention the book of Revelation or the longer ending of Mark (16:9-20). There is inserted in this latter addendum a reference to "this age of lawlessness and unbelief . . . under the sway of Satan" and the assertion that, after an allotted "term of years," there will be a time when sinners (perhaps even those who killed Jesus) will "sin no more" but "inherit the spiritual and incorruptible glory of righteousness, a glory which is in heaven."[76]

This sort of thinking in terms of eras to world history did not die out in the church in later centuries. It became fashionable for Christian historians, especially after Augustine, to trace out periods in history or a sequence of world empires. Later apocalyptists such as Joachim of Fiore worked with the idea of three ages — of the Father, of the Son, and of the Spirit.[77] Such schemes continue to flourish in our own day. A prominent example involves the "Dispensationalist Movement" ("dispensation" from *dispensatio,* the Latin counterpart to the Greek term *oikonomia*). Those associated with this movement maintain that God, who dispenses all things, has arranged different dispensations and has related (and continues to relate) to humanity in different ways at different times throughout history. The classic example of this approach is the *Scofield Reference Bible,* which specifies seven of these successive eras, or "dispensations," in which God has related to his people in essentially different ways.[78] Acceptance of this way of understanding history has come to be the hallmark of certain types of American fundamentalism.

It would be easy to look askance at the dispensationalist factor in considering stewardship-*oikonomia.* But a more positive response is possible: "modest dispensationalism," without the elaborate schemes of history and without the timetables of events before the end that some have built up. The point is this: all Christianity is, in a limited sense, dispensationalist. As a minimum, there is the fact that Christians speak of an Old Testament or Old Covenant and a New. (Even those who speak of "the Hebrew Scriptures" and Greek "New Testament" or of a "first Testament" and a "second Testament" have to face the theological question of how they relate these two bodies of writings.) The claim implicit in all such language is that, since Jesus, those who are "in Christ" stand on the threshold of the new age or live with feet and lives simultaneously in the old era and the new, or that the new is breaking in. "The appointed time has grown short . . . the present form of this world is passing away" (1 Cor. 7:29, 31, NRSV). Even though such eschatology has often been misunderstood, and the term "New Age" is today abused, Christianity would not be Christianity without some element of it. The new creaturehood of which Paul speaks (2 Cor. 5:17) is a reflection of the powers of the age to come already at work in us through baptism.

If we wish a more elaborate example of periodization in the New Testament, there is the pattern of heilsgeschichte that Luke presents, described above: the Age of Israel, the time of Jesus,

112

the Age of the Church. Such concepts have informed the faith of Christians throughout the history of the church.

Efforts to identify more dispensations (e.g., C. I. Scofield's seven) usually involve questionable exegesis and ultimately demonstrate a lack of trust in God. The interpreters apparently feel the need to map out the future definitively from what are but hints in Scripture, hints clear primarily to dispensationalists but often rigorously disputed among them. And as a matter of historical record, these predictions have often proved inaccurate. But the mind-set that sees a newness in Christ and a fulfillment into which we have entered, though not yet fully, not entirely, is a contribution to apocalypticism. Such a mind-set allows people to treasure God's continuing work in and for the future without abandoning hope and without rigidly codifying future expectations or "reifying" (or "thing-ifying") existing institutions by identifying them idolatrously with God's reign. Christians should "keep loose" about things that are not ultimate.

If one had to try to characterize, in a single phrase, the overall positive contribution of New Testament apocalypticism, one might say that it frees us for realistic planning and realization of goals under God. It introduces an element of "teleology" by reminding us that God's *telos* involves both the Deity's goal and the *finis* for human pretensions and plans. It adds a dimension to the two types of stewardship discussed above rather than presenting a third.

113

Applying the Rediscovered Word "Stewardship" in God's Economy

Our quest began with a question: What *is* stewardship? Just fund-raising, or a banner under which to try to integrate all of theology and ethics and whatever else catches the eye of church leaders or theologians currently?

My aim in this study has not been to attempt to define the term once and for all. That would not only be presumptuous but would run counter to the evidence we have considered about how varied the meanings and applications for the *oikonomia* family of words and their descendants have been over more than twenty centuries. Perhaps each church group and period of history must provide its own working definition. The effort here has been to aid this ongoing process by showing what the Greek word out of which the stewardship concept grew has meant over a long history.

A. Some Conclusions

To review, let us restate some of the points established in the preceding chapters.

1. A classical, Greco-Roman, often philosophical, but widespread and popular concept of the "economy of God" devel-

oped before the New Testament era and quite apart from the Bible.

2. While biblical use of *oikonomia* and related terms was limited, a New Testament base was established, especially in Paul, for later development.

3. The Church Fathers drew on *oikonomia* terminology in developing a concept of salvation history or heilsgeschichte, with a series of meanings richer than has usually been supposed.

4. During and after the patristic era, the concept of the economy of God associated with *oikonomia* terminology continued to intertwine with concepts of history in a number of ways.

5. From the Latin *dispensatio,* a frequent rendering of *oikonomia,* a later, tangentially related notion of "dispensationalism" grew up, occurring in both a proper and an exaggerated, sectarian way — on the one hand, two testaments, Luke's three ages; on the other, the elaborate dispensationalist schemes outlined in American fundamentalism.

6. Stewardship, as a church practice in search of a theology, is peculiarly North American and has had a checkered history. It has exhibited great vitality, especially in certain periods.

7. Christian stewardship has long been associated with "the story of salvation" as its heart. More recently, discussions have also begun to associate it with the notion of the creation as a divine gift. This latter association can provide Christians with a second incentive, alongside the gospel, to be good stewards, and it can provide the grounds for an appeal to all people, regardless of their religious background, to join one another for the common good on ecology, peace, and justice issues.

8. The apocalyptic (i.e., future-oriented) aspects of the biblical witness provide the basis for a necessary theological emphasis. The world of apocalyptic thinking sometimes provides the means for expressing hope in marginalized communities.

9. Ecumenical theology has begun to combine the classical theme of "the divine economy" and the modern emphasis on being "stewards."[1]

10. All this is to suggest, on the basis of historical, linguistic, and theological study, that there are certain core concerns as well as limitations to *oikonomia* / stewardship / *dispensatio* / the economy of God. No one image or definition can overarch all aspects of the *oikonomia* theme without diminishing the breadth and variety of the whole.

B. Two Bases for a Broader Stewardship

At this point it is appropriate to take a closer look at the two bases for stewardship mentioned in point 7 above. The primary basis lies in redemption. A Christian's self-understanding and stewardship outlook rest upon God's great act of redemption, which in the Hebrew Scriptures is the exodus from Egypt and in the New Testament is the cross of Jesus Christ (or cross and resurrection, or incarnation, or Christ event). But there is also a second basis for talking of identity, self-understanding, responsibility, and stewardship that is available for all peoples: creation, the initial work of God, originally developed in the Bible in light of redemption but later having a significance and import of its own. In almost all religions there is some concept of "beginnings," and there is usually some concept of ongoing divine providential care as well. In any case the concrete actuality of creation is all around every person, calling for decisions. More on that in a moment.

The sort of apocalyptic thought that we have explored in connection with stewardship and the divine economy (point 8, above) does not serve in quite the same way as a basis for appeals about identity, self-understanding, or stewardship. It is true that at times in the Bible and in subsequent centuries the apocalyptic tradition has built its outlook around what will happen when God acts finally and decisively. Such an appeal has power to this day to move the disenfranchised, those without hope, the prisoners of situations that are so bad that only divine intervention and judgment seem to provide a way out. But in reality apocalyptists (certainly those in the biblical tradition) usually have some knowledge of God's past acts of redemption and an awareness of God's role as Creator, even if they view the world of their own experience as hopelessly corrupt and the redemptive events so distant as not to be real amid present distresses. What happens in such instances is that faith functions as hope, offering assurance concerning the future and confidence of things not seen. The future hope and base for existence thus in a derived sense rest on experiences of redemption and creation. Christian theology has therefore always been somewhat wary of making the futurist argument its main appeal because of the conviction that the decisive intervention by God into human life has already come through Jesus Christ. One does not let the parousia become — in contrast to the cross, resurrection, or incarnation — the "tail that wags the dog."

Therefore it is the continuum of creation and redemption, with their pointers to and promise of a future consummation — the whole picture of beginning, middle, and end — that provides the basis for Christian living and thinking and therefore for stewardship. But now we must ask, Whose stewardship?

The somewhat unexpected biblical testimony is to *God's* stewardship, first and foremost, rather than ours. It is an economy of God, a plan of God, God's administration of the divine will, the work of God. It must be added, of course, that all such testimony, whether of Paul, Irenaeus, or some Old Testament

prophet, is an assertion of faith, not a bald philosophical propo-
sition, discernible to everyone.

There follows, of course, a "stewardship of all believers," to
use Hall's fine phrase. The biblical authors most convinced about
these matters do not call themselves "stewards of history," however, but, at most, "stewards of the mysteries of God" (1 Cor.
4:1), a phrase that refers to the role of the apostle and others in
preaching and advancing the gospel. As to stewarding "secular
history," obvious examples can be said to have occurred in the
Constantinian period, when avowedly Christian emperors sought
to reshape the Roman Empire, and later in such states as France
and Russia and Calvin's Geneva. Still, it is better to speak of
Christians as "stewards *in* history," holding fast to and carrying
out a heritage and a vision.

Were these stewards "history makers"? Sometimes, on large
scale or small, in bad ways or good (though admittedly judgment
of these points depends on standards that vary from person to
person). The list of those who made history in good ways might
include Josiah (at least the Deuteronomist thought so), David
(according to almost all biblical writers), Jeremiah (but not too
successfully by the world's standards), and Paul (though Jewish
authorities would have disagreed, and we know that some Jewish
Christians, including the author of the *Clementine Homilies* and
Recognitions, did not think so). On the other hand, most would
say that Ahab and Judas made history in a bad way. Yet some
modern scholars have read the records very differently. Norman
Gottwald, for example, has argued that Saul and David and all
their successors as king were a mistake and exemplified a tragic
turning away from the "golden era" of Israel's tribal period.[2]
Again, the irony of it all!

In a biblical sense, the real history maker, whether mentioned
in the historical record or not, turns out to be the individual who
has been faithful to God. How subsequent writers judge that
person depends in part on their definitions of God, history, and
stewardship.

C. Only for Christians?

Is stewardship then only for Christian believers? This was not an issue when the term meant simply fund-raising for ministry and missions or for other denominational programs. Of course only Christians, church members, and sympathizers did that. But the problem becomes acute when stewardship is stretched to include tackling a whole range of problems such as poverty, war and peace issues, and justice concerns. To deal with these on a national or global scale, one would need to draw on more than just the resources of the denominations that are members of the Canadian Interchurch Stewardship Committee, the National Council of the Churches of Christ in the U.S.A., or the Ecumenical Center for Stewardship Studies; in fact, one would need more than just the resources of all the churches of any sort that name the name of Christ. For world problems also involve and call for a response from Jews, Muslims, Hindus, Buddhists, and those who profess no religion or even an antipathy to religion.

To appeal to Christ (or to the exodus) as a central redemptive event limits the appeal to those in the Judeo-Christian tradition. It is impossible to speak of a broader stewardship when the core concept is based on christocentricity or the Trinity, as has often been the case.

It is the argument of this book that the history of the *oikonomia* theme shows a way out: Go back to the Greco-Roman historians and philosophers! There we met with the idea of an economy of God and a divine stewardship of history held by pre-Christian, non-Jewish writers. Concern for such an *oikonomia* could exist among pagans; indeed, it antedates Judeo-Christian development of the theme.

Such an approach fits well with the fact that today people all over the world have begun to use the word "stewardship" outside of ecclesiastical contexts, in the sense of "responsible use of resources" or wise management of what is at one's disposal. That sense does reflect certain connotations of the Greek word.

Put theologically, it is our argument that one can appeal to all prudent people to join, as their stewardship, in certain actions for the common good, not on the basis of "redemption" (which would apply only to believers) but on the basis of what we share in "creation" or "providentially."

To spell it out, if we are to deal with all or even just a significant portion of the things that people have lumped under stewardship, we will have to develop a twofold line of appeal. Both lines apply to Christians. The approach in light of creation applies to all women and men.

Creation	Redemption
There is a stewardship based on creation, justice, self-interest, creaturely concerns, self-love, and societal improvement. This endeavor is part of receiving life and being human at its fullest.	And there is a stewardship based on redemption, the gospel, God's saving righteousness, our response, and love to God, in ecclesial community. This endeavor comes from having received the Life of God's new age.

The twofold biblical use of the phrase "image of God" meshes also with these two approaches. All persons retain something of the *imago Dei;* "in Christ" believers possess it with promised fullness.

Apply this double line of reasoning to the case of cleaning up a polluted lake or cleansing the skies from acid rain. People who never darken the door of a church or who profess no adherence to any God have a stake in such matters out of pure self-interest and more altruistically for their children's sake. So do Christians, but Christians are also motivated by the fact that the lake and the skies are parts of God's world.

The course of action that Christians choose in specific instances may be exactly the same as that adopted by Jews,

121

Muslims, or atheists. It is the Christians' motive that would differ, for they better understand their place in God's creation and their status as redeemed children of God in Christ. If they grasp their gospel heritage, they possess an even more powerful motivation for getting involved — namely, the divine stewardship or plan of God in Christ, which has set us free to serve.

We have referred, alongside Christian stewardship, to a stewardship based on creation. This could be termed "Stoic stewardship," Islamic stewardship, or whatever. An appropriate name might be "worldly stewardship," since it is based on the world we share, and it is concerned for that world.

D. Church Tower Horizons?

Christians are sometimes criticized for having "church tower horizons" — they see no further than the church building and are less diligent than non-Christians when it comes to doing what needs to be done in the world that lies beyond them. Jesus may have implied as much when he said in passing that "the children of this age are more shrewd in dealing with their own generation than are the children of light" (Luke 16:8, NRSV). Christians who see no further than the church building and its steeple may need a broader outlook. It is true that the Christian vision and will to act have often been limited, that Christians have often been slower to respond to "worldly stewardship" needs than non-Christians. But the church tower may just offer a way to broaden the Christian outlook.

Many European church towers bears the symbol of a rooster, sometimes atop a weather vane on the church's spire, pointing to the four corners of God's world. The rooster figure is usually taken to symbolize Peter's denial of Jesus. When the cock crowed, Peter was reminded that Jesus had predicted his denial (Mark 14:30, 70-71). It stands therefore as a symbol of human sin and failure, even among leaders in a church community, the shortcomings of even the best. We live by forgiveness, as Peter discovered.

But the rooster symbol has a second meaning. The crowing of the rooster is also associated with the coming of the dawn (cf. Mark 13:35). Christians can see in this an ever new reminder of the first Easter morning and Christ's resurrection. In that paradigmatic redemptive event, God cut a window into the world. For Christians this symbol offers a view beyond all boundaries and barriers, even beyond death. It is an assertion that beyond all anguish is vindication and exaltation (a sense that speaks profoundly to the downtrodden). Beyond all time, Christ stands as the Lord over all creation. In this way, the church tower affords the view of a wider horizon, through Christ.

It is that view, looking out over all creation in the light of Easter, with an eye toward the end, that allows for a christocentric perspective on history, the world, and all of life for stewards in the divine economy.

The final question for each of us as we work at definitions, content, and practical applications of stewardship is whether we as individuals are in fact wise and faithful stewards. Both Jesus and Paul spoke in such terms about stewards (Luke 12:42; 1 Cor. 4:1-2). We are trustworthy disciples when we look at the whole creation in the light of God's work for us in Jesus Christ, the world, and gifts given to all humanity, aware that the God of Easter is working toward the goals of the divine purpose. The biblical good news is that believers have been given the opportunity to serve as stewards of the openly revealed gospel of God, to take part in a venture involving the many-sided wisdom and plan of God, as part of God's stewardship (Eph. 3:2, 9-10). The new insight is that all God's children, whether Christian or not, can have roles as stewards. All can join in stewardship, as part of God's economy.

Introduction

1. For the definitions cited, see, respectively, J. M. Versteeg, *The Deeper Meaning of Stewardship* (New York: Abingdon Press, 1923), p. 9; W. H. Greever, *Work of the Lord* (New York: Fleming H. Revell, 1937), p. 62; C. C. Stoughton, *Whatever You Do* (Philadelphia: Muhlenberg Press, 1949), p. 28; Alphin Carl Conrad, *The Divine Economy: A Study in Stewardship* (Grand Rapids: William B. Eerdmans, 1954), p. 27; and T. A. Kantonen, *A Theology for Christian Stewardship* (Philadelphia: Muhlenberg Press, 1956), pp. 9, 19, and "The Scriptural and Theological Basis of Evangelism and Stewardship," *Lutheran Quarterly* 3 (1951): 271-77. In the latter article, Kantonen outlines a trinitarian approach from the Creed:

> from the doctrine of creation we derive the concepts of God's sovereignty and our trusteeship and responsibility. From the doctrine of redemption we derive our insight into the grace which restores sinners into fellowship with God and awakens the gratitude, joy, and love which motivate us to give our lives to our Redeemer. From the doctrine of sanctification we derive our understanding of the living faith which, drawing upon God's resources, bears fruit in obedience and dedicated service. Faith in God the creator establishes evangelism and stewardship as God's work. Faith in God the Redeemer establishes the basis on which sinful men can do God's work. Faith in God the Sanctifier consecrates us to the doing of this work. (P. 277)

See also Wallace E. Fisher, *A New Climate for Stewardship* (Nashville: Abingdon Press, 1976), p. 21. There are additional definitions in Helge

Brattgård's book *God's Stewards: A Theological Study of the Principles and Practices of Stewardship,* trans. Gene J. Lund (Minneapolis: Augsburg Press, 1963), pp. 4-9; and Milo Kauffman's *Stewards of God* (Scottdale, Pa.: Herald Press, 1975), pp. 20-21.

2. Cited by Brattgård in *God's Stewards,* p. 5.

3. Brattgård offers the following understanding "commonly used" in the literature of the period: "Christian stewardship is the practice of systematic and proportionate giving of time, abilities, and material possessions, based on the conviction that these are trusts from God to be used in his service for the benefit of all mankind in grateful acknowledgment of Christ's redeeming love" (*God's Stewards,* p. 5).

4. *Twentieth Century Encyclopedia of Religious Knowledge,* vol. 2, ed. L. A. Loetscher (Grand Rapids: Baker Book House, 1955), p. 1062.

5. One cannot help but be aware of the strictures on the word-study method advanced in the early 1960s by James Barr in *The Semantics of Biblical Language* (New York: Oxford University Press, 1961) and by others. Without citing any of the enormous bibliography on the issue, I would simply note that I join many others (including Barr in some of his own later work) in viewing the method as one way to get at meanings so long as it is used with historical and methodological care. One recent trend is to examine the whole related "word field" of terms, which in this instance would center on the Greek word for "house" *(oikos, oikia)*.

6. For details see any good concordance of the Bible in its various translations. The 1611 Bible has *stewardship* at Luke 16:2, 3, and 4; *steward* at Gen. 15:2; 43:19; 44:1, 4; Matt. 20:8; Luke 8:3; 12:42; 16:1, 2 (verb, "be steward"), 3, 8; and Titus 1:7. The plural, *stewards,* occurs at 1 Chron. 28:1; 1 Cor. 4:1, 2; and 1 Pet. 4:10. At Matt. 20:8 and Luke 8:3 the Greek term is not *oikonomos* but *epitropos.* The RSV keeps all these KJV occurrences of *steward* terminology except Gen. 15:2 and adds the word in English at John 2:8-9 ("steward of the feast," Greek *architriklinos*); Isa. 22:15; Dan. 1:11, 16; Gen. 43:16; 44:1; and 1 Chron. 27:31; plus Eph. 3:2, "stewardship." The NEB employs "steward" somewhat less, preferring "bailiff" and "manager" at Luke 16:1, 2, 3, and 8. The NRSV (1991) follows the RSV but prefers "manager" in Luke 16, Matt. 20:8, and Luke 12:42; "guard" in Dan. 1; and "commission" at Eph. 3:2.

7. Anglo-Saxon *stigu + weard. Stigu* is usually understood to mean "cattle-pen," though its relationship to "sty," as in "pigsty," seems clear; see Kantonen, *A Theology of Christian Stewardship,* p. 3, or *Stewardship in Contemporary Theology,* Library of Christian Stewardship, ed. T. K. Thompson (New York: Association Press, 1960), p. ix. On the other hand, the *Oxford English Dictionary* suggests that *stig* "probably" means "house, hall," and *stig* and *sty* may be synonymous, but "there is no ground for the assumption that *stig weard* originally meant 'keeper of the the pig-sties'" (*OED,* 2d ed. [1989], 16: 664).

Chapter I

1. *Xenophon: Memorabilia and Oeconomicus,* Loeb Classical Library, trans. E. C. Marchant (London: Heinemann, 1923).

2. See Plato, *Laws* (5.747A; 7.808B, 809C, and 819C) and *Republic* (417A); Aristotle, *Politics* (1.1.2-3, 9, 21 [1252a 8-24; 1253a 2-4; 1255b 19-21]) and *Nicomachean Ethics* (1.1.3 [1094a 9]; 1.2.6 [1094b 2-3]; 6.8.3-4 [1141b 30-33, 1142a 9-10]), among other references.

3. *Aristotle: Metaphysics X-XVI, Oeconomica and Magna Moralia,* Loeb Classical Library, trans. C. G. Armstrong (London: Heinemann, 1935).

4. Philodemus, *Peri oikonomias,* ed. C. Jensen (Leipzig: Teubner, 1906). There is no English translation.

5. See O. Michel, *"oikos, oikia,"* *Theological Dictionary of the New Testament,* 8 vols., ed. G. Kittel and G. Friedrich, trans. G. W. Bromiley (Grand Rapids: Eerdmans, 1964-74), 5: 119-59; Abraham Malherbe, *Social Aspects of Early Christianity,* 2d ed. (Philadelphia: Fortress Press, 1983), especially pp. 60-92; Robert Banks, *Paul's Idea of Community: The Early House Churches in Their Historical Setting* (Grand Rapids: William B. Eerdmans, 1980); John H. Elliott, *A Home for the Homeless: A Sociological Exegesis of 1 Peter, Its Situation and Strategy* (Philadelphia: Fortress Press, 1981); and Vincent P. Branick, *The House Church in the Writings of Paul,* Zacchaeus Studies (Wilmington, Del.: Michael Glazier, 1989). It has been estimated that in the Roman port city of Ostia less than 10 percent of the people lived in private homes and multistory apartments, 20 percent were on the streets, and 70 percent in one- or two-room apartments; see James E. Packer, *The Insulae of Imperial Ostia,* Memoirs of the American Academy of Rome 31 (Rome: American Academy in Rome, 1971), pp. 70-71. On Corinth, see Jerome Murphy-O'Connor, *St. Paul's Corinth: Texts and Archaeology,* Good News Studies 6 (Wilmington, Del.: Michael Glazier, 1983).

6. See James E. Crouch, *The Origin and Intention of the Colossian Haustafeln,* Forschungen zur Religion und Literatur des Alten und Neuen Testaments 109 (Göttingen: Vandenhoeck & Ruprecht, 1972); Elliott, *Home for the Homeless;* David L. Balch, *Let Wives Be Submissive: The Domestic Code in 1 Peter,* Society of Biblical Literature Monograph Series 26, 2d ed. (Chico, Cal.: Scholars Press, 1988); David C. Verner, *The Household of God: The Social World of the Pastoral Epistles,* Society of Biblical Literature Dissertation Series 71 (Chico, Cal.: Scholars Press, 1983).

7. See Max L. Stackhouse, "What Shall We Do? On Using Scripture in Economic Ethics," *Interpretation* 41 (1987): 382-97. See especially pp. 394-97 on *oikos* and *polis* with reference to justice.

8. J. Reumann, " 'Stewards of God' — Pre-Christian Religious Application of *oikonomos* in Greek," *Journal of Biblical Literature* 77 (1958): 339-49.

9. J. Reumann, "OIKONOMIA = 'Covenant': Terms for Heilsge-schichte in Early Christian Usage," *Novum Testamentum* 3 (1959): 282-92.

10. On the recent revival of rhetoric in connection with biblical studies, see Burton L. Mack, *Rhetoric and the New Testament,* Guides to Biblical Scholarship, New Testament Series (Minneapolis: Fortress Press, 1990).

11. J. Reumann, *"Oikonomia* as 'Ethical Accommodation' in the Fathers and Its Pagan Background," in *Studia Patristica III,* ed. F. L. Cross, Texte und Untersuchungen 78 (Berlin: Akademie-Verlag, 1961), pp. 370-79.

12. Brattgård, *God's Stewards: A Theological Study of the Principles and Practices of Stewardship,* trans. Gene J. Lund (Minneapolis: Augsburg Press, 1963), pp. 42-44; Hall, *The Steward: A Biblical Symbol Come of Age* (New York: Friendship Press, 1982), p. 14.

13. Sheef, "Stewardship in the Old Testament," in *Stewardship in Contemporary Theology,* Library of Christian Stewardship, ed. T. K. Thompson (New York: Association Press, 1960), pp. 17-38.

14. Scott C. Layton has examined possible Mesopotamian and Egyptian origins for this term, which appears in the Joseph story (Gen. 37–50) and 2 Kings and Isaiah (in the administrative structuring under David and Solomon). He concludes that "the Israelite office of royal steward" was patterned "after the administrative traditions of Canaanite city-states" ("The Steward in Ancient Israel: A Study of the Hebrew [*ʾăšer*] *ʿal-habbayit* in Its Near Eastern Setting," *Journal of Biblical Literature* 109 [1990]: 649).

15. It was transliterated as *ʾiqonomos* (איקונומוס); see M. Jastrow, *A Dictionary to the Targumim, the Talmud Babli and Yerushalmi and the Midrashic Literature* (Berlin: Verlag Choreb, 1926), p. 60.

16. For exegetical treatment, see J. Reumann, *Jesus in the Church's Gospels: Modern Scholarship and the Earliest Sources* (Philadelphia: Fortress Press, 1968), pp. 189-98; and J. Fitzmyer, *The Gospel According to Luke X–XXIV,* Anchor Bible 28A (Garden City, N.Y.: Doubleday, 1985), pp. 1094-1111. While Douglas E. Oakman does not dwell on Luke 16:1-8, he does engage recent "sociological consciousness" approaches to the Gospels (*Jesus and the Economic Questions of His Day,* Studies in the Bible and Early Christianity 8 (Lewiston, N.Y.: Edwin Mellen Press, 1986). Oakman concludes that Jesus ran counter to the tendencies of the day toward exploitation, patronage, and centralization of power in urging decentralization, redistribution of goods to satisfy human needs, and "reciprocity," or the giving of gifts. Jesus' parables were populated with "middle" people such as the steward of the estate in 16:1-8, who, according to Oakman, are "a key ingredient to changing the situation." For more on Oakman's method, see "The Ancient Economy in the Bible," *Biblical Theology Bulletin* 21 (1991): 34-39. Of course this approach faces not only the hazards of the "quest" for the historical Jesus but also issues in sociological and economic interpretation.

17. See Cadbury, *Jesus — What Manner of Man* (London: SPCK, 1962), pp. 23-31; cf. Fitzmyer, *Luke X–XXIV,* pp. 983-93. Space does not

permit exploring church structures involving the household here. These include the "house church" (for literature, see note 5 above), the church as the "household *(oikos)* of the living God" (1 Tim. 3:15), and the bishop as *oikonomos,* or "God's steward" (Tit. 1:7). For some aspects of this development, see J. Reumann, *Variety and Unity in New Testament Thought* (New York: Oxford University Press, 1991), pp. 139-48. For a treatment of the household *(oikia)* theme in the Gospel of Matthew, see Michael H. Crosby, *House of Disciples: Church, Economics, and Justice in Matthew* (Maryknoll, N.Y.: Orbis Books, 1988), pp. 21-75, 99-125.

18. See Reumann, " 'Stewards of God' — Pre-Christian Religious Application of *oikonomos* in Greek."

19. See G. Bornkamm, *"mystērion,"* *Theological Dictionary of the New Testament,* 4: 802-27; and Raymond E. Brown, *The Semitic Background of the Term "Mystery" in the New Testament,* Facet Books Biblical Series 21 (Philadelphia: Fortress Press, 1968).

20. Polybius, *The Histories,* trans. W. R. Paton, Loeb Classical Library, 6 vols. (Cambridge: Harvard University Press, 1922-27), 1: 8-11.

21. A. H. McDonald, "Polybius," *The Oxford Classical Dictionary,* ed. M. Cary et al. (Oxford: Clarendon Press, 1949), p. 711; cf. F. F. Walbank's article on Polybius in the second edition of the *Oxford Classical Dictionary* (Oxford: Clarendon Press, 1970), pp. 853-54.

22. *Diodorus of Sicily,* trans. C. H. Oldfather, Loeb Classical Library, 10 vols. (Cambridge: Harvard University Press, 1933-54), 3: 96-97.

23. Dionysius of Halicarnassus, *On Thucydides* 9, trans. W. K. Pritchett (Berkeley and Los Angeles: University of California Press, 1975); *Critical Essays, I: On the Ancient Orators,* trans. S. Usher, Loeb Classical Library (Cambridge: Harvard University Press, 1985).

24. See George A. Kennedy, *New Testament Interpretation through Rhetorical Criticism* (Chapel Hill, N.C.: University of North Carolina Press, 1984).

25. See, for example, McDonald, "Polybius," p. 711.

26. H. J. Rose, *A Handbook of Greek Literature,* 3d ed. (London: Methuen, 1948), p. 371; cf. Polybius, *The Histories* 29.21.

27. K. Ziegler, "Polybios," in *Real-Encyclopaedie der classischen Altertumswissenschaft,* ed. A. Pauly, C. Wissowa, and W. Kroll (Stuttgart: Druckenmüller, 1894-1938), 21/2: 1440-1578, esp. pp. 1516, 1532-43. Cf. Ziegler's "Polybios," in *Der Kleine Pauly,* vol. 4 (Stuttgart: Druckenmüller, 1964-75), pp. 982-91, especially pp. 984-89.

28. See Polybius, *The Histories* 10.5.8.

29. See *De fortuna Romanorum,* in Plutarch's *Moralia* 316B-26C, trans. F. C. Babbitt, vol. 4, Loeb Classical Library (Cambridge: Harvard University Press, 1936), pp. 319-78.

30. Fowler, "Polybius' Conception of *Tyche,"* *Classical Review* 17 (1903): 448.

31. See H. F. Pelham's article on "Polybius" in the eleventh edition of the *Encyclopaedia Britannica* (1910-11), 22: 19, col. b.

32. For discussion of the Stoic notion of the "divine economy," especially in relation to later Christianity, see Edwin Hatch, *The Influence of Greek Ideas and Usages upon the Christian Church,* 2d ed., ed. A. M. Fairbairn (1901; rpt., New York: Harper Torchbooks, 1957); and G. L. Prestige, *God in Patristic Thought,* 2d ed. (London: SPCK, 1952).

Chapter II

1. Hatch, *The Influence of Greek Ideas and Usages upon the Christian Church,* 2d ed., ed. A. M. Fairbairn (1901; rpt., New York: Harper Torchbooks, 1957).

2. Prestige, *God in Patristic Thought,* 2d ed. (London: SPCK, 1952).

3. *A Patristic Greek Lexicon,* ed. G. W. H. Lampe (Oxford: Clarendon Press, 1961-63), pp. 940-44, 1565-67.

4. Cf. Hatch, *The Influence of Greek Ideas and Usages upon the Christian Church,* pp. 217-32.

5. See the references to Origen's commentaries on the Gospels and Eusebius's *Church History* 10.4.46 in Lampe, *A Patristic Greek Lexicon,* p. 942.

6. See Prestige, *God in Patristic Thought,* pp. 97-111. The "economic Trinity" stressed a dispensational revelation of God in stages, first in the Logos and then in the Spirit, rather than an ontological emphasis on common "essence" or being. This view developed and was maintained by many during the first three or four centuries of the Christian era. Such a notion was held, for example, by Sabellius concerning the Father, the Son, and the Spirit as successive forms or "persons" *(prosōpa)* of the Godhead. Unity was maintained at the expense of identity in essence. It was, we may say, "emanationist."

7. Prestige, *God in Patristic Thought,* p. 62.

8. See J. Reumann, *"Oikonomia* as 'Ethical Accommodation' in the Fathers and Its Pagan Background," in *Studia Patristica III,* ed. F. L. Cross, Texte und Untersuchungen 78 (Berlin: Akademie-Verlag, 1961), pp. 370-79.

9. John Chrysostom, "Commentary on Galatians," in *Nicene and Post-Nicene Fathers of the Christian Church* [hereafter NPNF], series 1, 14 vols., ed. Philip Schaff (Buffalo and New York: Christian Literature, 1886-1890), 13: 18-20. *Oikonomia* is translated as "a scheme" and "plan." In a note on p. 19, Gross Alexander, who revised the anonymous Oxford rendering, adds that "in earlier life Chrysostom had himself practised such a 'scheme' as that which he here attributes to Paul," of tendering a falsehood for a good purpose.

10. Patrides, *The Grand Design of God: The Literary Form of the Christian View of History* (London: Routledge & Kegan Paul, 1972).

11. This is the broad conclusion of the 1955 Erlangen dissertation by Otto Lillge, "Das patristische Wort *oikonomia,* seine Geschichte und Bedeutung bis auf Origenes"; cf. *Theologisches Literaturzeitung* 80 (1955): 239.

12. See J. Reumann, " 'Jesus the Steward': An Overlooked Theme in Christology," in *Studia Evangelica V,* ed. F. L. Cross, Texte und Untersuchungen 103 (Berlin: Akademie-Verlag, 1968), pp. 21-29.

13. See especially the summaries in Prestige, *God in Patristic Thought,* pp. 55-75, 98-102.

14. Justin Martyr, *Dialogue* 107.3 (in J. P. Migne, *Patrologia Graeca* [hereafter, *PG*] 6.725A); Chrysostom, *Homilies on Ephesians* 6.2 (*PG* 11.40E).

15. Eusebius, *Ecclesiastical History* 2.2.6.

16. See Irenaeus, *Against Heresies* 4.31.1 (*PG* 7.1068C); Justin Martyr, *Dialogue* 134.2 (*PG* 6.785C).

17. William R. Schoedel, *Ignatius of Antioch,* Hermeneia (Philadelphia: Fortress Press, 1985), pp. 84-85.

18. On Ignatius, *Eph.* 6.1, see Schoedel, *Ignatius of Antioch,* pp. 54, 56n.15. For references to events in Christ's life, see Lampe's *Patristic Greek Lexicon,* s.v. *oikonomia,* C.6.f. (p. 942).

19. Antiochus Ptolemaieus, *Homilia in Adam,* p. 652, cited by Lampe in *A Patristic Greek Lexicon,* p. 942; Irenaeus, *Against Heresies* 1.14.6 (*PG* 7.608A).

20. *Apophthegmata Patrum* ("Sayings of the Fathers"), *Abb. Mac.* 2, cited by Prestige in *God in Patristic Thought,* p. 66.

21. Joannes Moschus, *Pratum spirituale* 83 (*PG* 87/3.2852).

22. Eusebius, *Ecclesiastical History* 2.2.6.

23. Prestige, *God in Patristic Thought,* p. 67.

24. See Prestige, *God in Patristic Thought,* p. 66. For further examples, see Lampe, *A Patristic Greek Lexicon,* s.v. *oikonomia* C.4 (p. 941). The Epiphanius reference is to his *Panarion,* or *Against Heresies* 75.3 (*PG* 42.505C).

25. Schoedel, *Ignatius of Antioch,* p. 96.

26. Gregory of Nazianzus, *Orationes* 42.13 *(PG* 36.473A).

27. The *Ecclesiastical History* is readily available in the Loeb Classical Library, ed. K. Lake, 2 vols. (London: Heinemann, 1926, 1932). A translation of the *Vita Constantini* by E. C. Richardson appears in NPNF, series 2, 14 vols. (New York: Christian Literature, 1890-1900), 1: 481-540. The *Praeparatio Evangelica* (*PG* 21) was translated by E. H. Gifford in 2 vols. (Oxford: Oxford University Press, 1903). *Saint Irenaeus, Proof of the Apostolic Preaching* appears in the Ancient Christian Writers series, no. 16, ed. Joseph P. Smith (Westminster, Md.: Newman, 1952). Among the many other writings of Eusebius was his *Chronicle,* which survives only in fragments but which was of great influence.

28. Milburn, *Early Christian Interpretations of History* (London: A. & C. Black, 1954), p. 54. On Eusebius, see also Robert L. Wilken, *The Myth of Christian Beginnings: History's Impact on Belief* (Garden City, N.Y.: Doubleday, 1971), pp. 52-76; and Glenn F. Chestnut, "Eusebius: The History of Salvation from the Garden of Eden to the Rise of the Roman Empire," in *The First Christian Historians* (Macon, Ga.: Mercer University Press, 1986), pp. 66-95, reprinted in *The Christian and Judaic Invention of History,* ed. Jacob Neusner, American Academy of Religion Studies on Religion 55 (Atlanta: Scholars Press, 1990), pp. 77-102. The essays gathered by Neusner seek to argue that "history was reinvented" from the fourth century on, after the Constantinian establishment, first by Christians, then by Jews. This is not to deny that previously people wrote history; rather it is to argue that historical reflections in writing began at this point to take a narrative form, "the representation of intelligible sequences of purposeful events presented as narrative" (pp. 3-4). By beginning with an excerpt from Burton Mack's *A Myth of Innocence* (Philadelphia: Fortress Press, 1987), the Neusner volume produces the effect for Christians of shifting accounts about "the beginnings of things" from the historical Jesus to a later " 'foundational' stratum" — not that of Constantine's day but to the evangelists' foundational Gospels, notably Mark's (pp. 19-20). But even if Luke and Hegesippus are historians of sorts, according to Wilken, Eusebius is "the rightful 'father of church history' " (*The Myth of Christian Beginnings,* p. 52). It was history as written in the fourth and fifth centuries that sought a "pattern of events" which made identity possible. "From Constantine onward, . . . Judaism . . . as well as the main stream of Christianity identified history as the foundational mode of thought and discourse" (Neusner, *The Christian and Judaic Invention of History,* p. 4). In neither of these volumes, however, does one encounter the *oikonomia* theme. The claims of Hans Frei and others (see Chap. 4, note 2 below) for a traditional Christian narrative as story of salvation in the Bible and over the centuries must wrestle with the Neusner volume on the development in the fourth century of such a specific "history-like" narrative and, in a different vein, with Wilken's iconoclasm over how religious groups develop myths about their origins.

29. Eusebius, *Ecclesiastical History* 5.1.32.

30. Eusebius, *Ecclesiastical History* 7.11.2.

31. Patrides, *The Grand Design of God,* p. 16.

32. Hall, "Mission as a Function of Stewardship," in *Spotlighting Stewardship* (Don Mills, Ont.: United Church of Canada, 1981), pp. 21-28; and *The Steward: A Biblical Symbol Come of Age* (New York: Friendship Press, 1982), pp. 34-37.

33. *Historiarum Adversum Paganos* (in J. P. Migne, *Patrologia Latina* [hereafter *PL*] 31); ET, Irving Woodworth Raymond, *Seven Books of History* (New York: Columbia University Press, 1936).

34. Patrides, *The Grand Design of God,* p. 19.

35. See Milburn, *Early Christian Interpretations of History,* p. 90.

36. *PL* 20: 95-460; ET in NPNF, series 2, 11: 71-122.

37. Gibbon, *The Decline and Fall of the Roman Empire,* ed. J. B. Bury (1897), 3: 266n. and 153n., respectively, as cited by Patrides in *The Grand Design of God,* p. 20.

38. Salvian of Marseilles, *De gubernatione Dei* 3.1 (*PL* 53: 55-56); ET, *On the Government of God,* trans. E. M. Sanford, Records of Civilization, Sources and Studies 12 (New York: Columbia University Press, 1930). For more on this, see Milburn, *Early Christian Interpretations of History,* pp. 92-95. Pagan virtues are contrasted with Roman vices in defending the work of providence.

39. Salvian of Marseilles, *De gubernatione Dei* 1.6 (*PG* 53: 51).

40. Salvian of Marseilles, *De gubernatione Dei* 2.1 (*PG* 53: 47).

41. See Patrides, *The Grand Design of God,* p. 21.

42. Augustine, *De Civitate Dei* (*PL* 41); ET NPNF, series 1, vol. 2.

43. For Otto of Freising, see the text edited by Adolf Hofmeister (Hannover/Leipzig, 1912, in the Scriptores Rerum Germanicarum in Usum Scholarum series) and the translation *The Two Cities,* by C. C. Mierow in the Records of Civilization, Sources and Studies (New York: Columbia University Press, 1928). Paris's *Chronica* has been edited by H. R. Luard (1872-83).

44. Patrides contends that "the finest exposition of the Christian view of history" in the thousand years after Augustine occurs in Dante's *Divine Comedy* (*The Grand Design of God,* p. 39).

45. Hall, *The Steward,* pp. 37-38.

46. See Cohn, *The Pursuit of the Millennium,* rev. ed. (London: Secker & Warburg, 1970).

47. Joachim of Fiore, *Liber concordiae novi ac veteris testamenti; Expositio in apocalypsim;* and *Psalterium decem cordatum.* For studies of his work, see, for example, Marjorie Reeves, *The Influence of Prophecy in the Later Middle Ages* (Oxford: Clarendon Press, 1969); Delno C. West, *Joachim of Fiore: A Study in Spiritual Perception and History* (Bloomington, Ind.: Indiana University Press, 1983); and Bernard McGinn, *The Calabrian Abbot: Joachim of Fiore in the History of Western Thought* (New York: Macmillan, 1985). See also n. 77 in Chapter V.

48. See Patrides, *The Grand Design of God,* p. 31.

49. See Patrides, *The Grand Design of God,* pp. 48-50. I would, however, take issue with Patrides's assertion that "crucial to the Protestant interpretation of history was the acceptance of the Book of Revelation as prophetic of actual events" of the day (p. 50) and, indeed, that this focus was "sanctioned by Luther" (p. 61n.15). This flies in the face of the fact that Luther gave the Apocalypse a lesser place within the canon, putting it on unnumbered pages in his 1522 New Testament. He did not exclude the book from the canon, to be sure, but he did put it in a class with other books

to which he assigned a lesser rank. Patrides further calls attention, in the footnote cited, to the development, in the seventeenth century, of an extreme apocalyptic militantism that looked for a "Fifth Monarchy" — that is, a kingdom that would supersede the four kingdoms prophesied in the book of Daniel. If this fits Hall's tradition of the "thin line" of "the disinherited," it also shows that their views were fueled by apocalyptic ideas again and again. On Luther, see Paul Althaus, *The Theology of Martin Luther* (Philadelphia: Fortress Press, 1966), pp. 418-25.

50. Patrides sees this view of history lingering far longer in America than in Europe, with "progress" as a secularized form of millennial expectations (*The Grand Design of God,* pp. 124-35). But the transformed "grand design" of the traditional Christian view of history can be found in the writings of William Blake ("the history of the destruction of innocence"), Wordsworth (*The Prelude* as a redemptive process in life and history, without Christ), and other cyclical-minded Romantics. T. S. Eliot, especially in the *Four Quartets,* shows that "the fabric of the Christian view of history has not utterly dissolved, nor its pageant faded."

51. See Patrides, *The Grand Design of God,* p. 218. To those who saw a visitation of divine justice in the 1 November 1755 earthquake, Voltaire put the question of why Lisbon was destroyed while Paris was allowed to dance on.

Chapter III

1. Some surveys of this considerable variety of perspectives appear in the notes below. In addition, see the essays in *History and Historical Understanding,* ed. C. T. McIntire and Ronald A. Wells (Grand Rapids: William B. Eerdmans, 1984). For the examples just mentioned, see Christopher Dawson, *The Dynamics of World History,* ed. J. J. Mulloy (New York: Sheed & Ward, 1956); Martin D'Arcy, *The Meaning and Matter of History: A Christian View* (New York: Farrar, Straus & Giroux, 1959); Reinhold Niebuhr, *Faith and History: A Comparison of Christian and Modern Views of History* (New York: Scribner's, 1949); and Paul Tillich, *The Interpretation of History* (New York: Scribner's, 1936). For the claim that history bears the largest number of meanings that we can know and the thesis that confidence in the noetic possibilities of history is inseparable from confidence in the central assertions of dogmatic theology — and hence that the link between a vital theory of history and the premises of Christian dogmatic theology is itself a singular historical process — see Paul Merkley, *The Greek and Hebrew Origins of Our Idea of History,* Toronto Studies in Theology 32 (Lewiston, N.Y.: Edwin Mellen Press, 1988).

2. Collingwood, *The Idea of History* (Oxford: Clarendon Press, 1946).

3. *Gaudium et Spes* ("Joy and Hope," the opening words in Latin of

the Constitution *De Ecclesia*) appears in translation in *The Documents of Vatican II,* ed. Walter M. Abbott (New York: Association Press, 1966), pp. 199-318. See pp. 247-48 for §45. "God in Nature and History" can be found in *New Directions in Faith and Order, Bristol 1967: Reports —Minutes — Documents,* Faith and Order Paper No. 50 (Geneva: World Council of Churches, 1968), pp. 7-31; see especially pp. 24-30.

4. Wright, *God Who Acts* (London: SCM Press, 1952); and *The Old Testament against Its Environment,* Studies in Biblical Theology (SBT) 2 (London: SCM Press, 1950). Filson, *The New Testament against Its Environment: The Gospel of Christ the Risen Lord,* SBT 3 (London: SCM Press, 1950). G. E. Wright and Reginald H. Fuller, *The Book of the Acts of God: Christian Scholarship Interprets the Bible,* Christian Faith Series, ed. Reinhold Niebuhr (Garden City, N.Y.: Doubleday, 1957).

5. Sittler, "Called to Unity," *The Ecumenical Review* 14 (1961-62): 177-87. See also the discussion of Col. 1:15-20, especially with regard to the Indian setting, in J. Reumann, *Creation and New Creation: The Past, Present, and Future of God's Creative Activity* (Minneapolis: Augsburg Press, 1973), pp. 42-56.

6. See M. Howard Rienstra, "Christianity and History: A Bibliographical Essay," in *A Christian View of History?* ed. George Marsden and Frank Roberts (Grand Rapids: William B. Eerdmans, 1975), p. 184. See also William A. Speck, "Kenneth Scott Latourette's Vocation as Christian Historian," in *A Christian View of History,* pp. 119-37.

7. William A. Speck, "Herbert Butterfield: The Legacy of a Christian Historian," in *A Christian View of History?* p. 101. On Butterfield's career, see *Herbert Butterfield: Writings on Christianity and History,* ed. C. T. McIntire (New York: Oxford University Press, 1979); on the Cambridge lectures, see p. 15.

8. See Butterfield, *Christianity and History* (New York: Scribner's, 1949), pp. 49-50, where he asserts that the years 1918, 1933, and 1945 constitute "a valid example of moral judgment within . . . history." See also pp. 74-75, 103, where he compares the events in Germany with the English art of "muddling through." Subsequent references to this volume will be made parenthetically in the text, using the abbreviation *CH.*

9. "God came without a sound," wrote Butterfield. "He was an elf. Quickly he disappeared" (*Herbert Butterfield: Writings on Christianity and History,* p. xxiv).

10. See *Herbert Butterfield: Writings on Christianity and History,* p. xxviii.

11. See Speck, "Herbert Butterfield: The Legacy of a Christian Historian," p. 116.

12. Löwith, "History and Christianity," in *Reinhold Niebuhr: His Religious, Social, and Political Thought,* ed. C. W. Kegley and R. W. Bretall (New York: Macmillan, 1956), p. 290.

13. See Ritschl, *The Christian Doctrine of Justification and Reconciliation,* trans. H. R. Mackintosh and A. B. Macaulay (New York: Scribner's, 1900). Ritschl juxtaposed his view of Jesus' message about the kingdom with the Reformation's emphasis on justification by faith.

14. See Weiss, *Jesus' Proclamation of the Kingdom of God,* trans. and ed. R. H. Hiers and D. L. Holland (Philadelphia: Fortress Press, 1971); and Schweitzer, *The Quest of the Historical Jesus,* trans. W. Montgomery (1910; repr., New York: Macmillan, 1968).

15. Gilkey, *Reaping the Whirlwind: A Christian Interpretation of History* (New York: Seabury Press, 1976), p. 217; cf. pp. 216-26.

16. Löwith, *Meaning in History: The Theological Implications of the Philosophy of History* (Chicago: University of Chicago Press, 1950), pp. 191-203.

17. So Frank Roberts in *A Christian View of History?* pp. 12-13.

18. See Rienstra, "Christianity and History," pp. 188-89; and Van A. Harvey, *The Historian and the Believer: The Morality of Historical Knowledge and Christian Belief* (New York: Macmillan, 1966), p. 38.

19. Bultmann, *History and Eschatology* (Edinburgh: University Press, 1957), p. 155.

20. On the distinction between *Historie* and *Geschichte,* see Gilkey, *Reaping the Whirlwind,* pp. 402-3 and n. 74. *Historie* with its adjective *historisch,* from the Latin *historia,* has come to mean, in this contrast, "historical," referring to past history, often with the sense of verifiably objective history, while *Geschichte* with its adjective *geschichtlich,* of German derivation, is taken to refer to that which is "historic" — that is, having happened in the past but with meaning for today, "existential-historical." Cf. Rienstra, "Christianity and History," pp. 191-94.

21. Löwith, *Meaning in History,* p. 195; cf. pp. 184-207.

22. Gilkey, *Reaping the Whirlwind,* p. 224.

23. See, e.g., Hall, *The Steward: A Biblical Symbol Come of Age* (New York: Friendship Press, 1982), p. 61.

24. See Hall, *Lighten Our Darkness: Toward an Indigenous Theology of the Cross* (Philadelphia: Westminster Press, 1976).

25. See Hall, *The Steward,* pp. 66ff.; and *Imaging God: Dominion as Stewardship* (Grand Rapids: William B. Eerdmans, 1986), pp. 181, 188-89.

26. See Hall, *The Steward,* pp. 61-63.

27. Hall, *The Steward,* p. 62.

28. See, e.g., Hall, *Christian Mission: The Stewardship of Life in the Kingdom of Death* (New York: Friendship Press, 1985), pp. 8, 11-12, 17-18, 79.

29. See, e.g., Hall, *The Steward,* p. 81.

30. Johnson, "Three Perspectives on the Church and Possessions," videotaped presentation at the Pennsylvania Northeast Conference Continuing Education Event, United Church of Christ, 15 January 1986.

31. See Brattgård, *God's Stewards: A Theological Study of the Principles and Practices of Stewardship,* trans. Gene J. Lund (Minneapolis: Augsburg Press, 1963), pp. 4, 8-9, 18; and Kantonen, *A Theology for Christian Stewardship* (Philadelphia: Muhlenberg Press, 1956), p. 4.

32. Azariah's *Christian Giving* was first published in English in 1939. A revised edition was published by Association Press in 1955 as a part of the World Christian Books series, with a foreword by T. K. Thompson and an expression of appreciation by the series editor, Stephen Neill; it was bound together with the first four titles in the series as *New Power to Witness,* in a Pulpit Book Club edition.

33. Salstrand, *The Story of Stewardship in the United States of America* (Grand Rapids: Baker Book House, 1956). The author was Professor of New Testament Interpretation and Evangelism at Tennessee Temple Schools, Chattanooga.

34. See Salstrand, *The Story of Stewardship in the United States of America,* pp. 13-26.

35. See Salstrand, *The Story of Stewardship in the United States of America,* pp. 26-27. See also Bacon, *The Christian Doctrine of Stewardship with Respect to Property* (New Haven: Nathan Whiting, 1832); and Finney, *Lectures to Professing Christians* (New York: John W. Taylor, 1837).

36. Cited by Salstrand in *The Story of Stewardship in the United States of America,* p. 33.

37. See Salstrand, *The Story of Stewardship in the United States of America,* pp. 41-46.

38. The principles were explained in a book by James A. Hensey entitled *Storehouse Tithing; or, Stewardship Up-to-Date* (New York: Fleming H. Revell, 1922). See Salstrand, *The Story of Stewardship in the United States of America,* pp. 42-43.

39. Lansdell, *The Sacred Tenth; or, Studies in Tithe-Giving Ancient and Modern,* 2 vols. (1906; repr., Grand Rapids: Baker Book House, 1954). A revised edition was published under the title *The Tithe in Scripture, Being Chapters from "The Sacred Tenth," with a Revised Bibliography on Tithe-Giving and Systematic and Proportionate Giving* (London: SPCK, 1908).

40. See Salstrand, *The Story of Stewardship in the United States of America,* pp. 47-76.

41. For a discussion of how the stewardship movement cut across denominational lines, see Salstrand, *The Story of Stewardship in the United States of America,* pp. 47-52; for a description of the Interchurch World Movement appeal of 1919-22 and its general failure, see pp. 63-64.

42. Volumes that have appeared in the Library of Christian Stewardship include the following: T. A. Kantonen, *Stewardship in Contemporary Theology* (New York: Association Press, 1960); *Christian Stewardship and Ecumenical Confrontation* (a collection of lectures presented at a consultation of the World Council of Churches Department on the Laity and the

Ecumenical Institute at Bossey, published by the NCCCUSA/Department of Stewardship and Benevolence, 1961); T. K. Thompson, *Handbook of Stewardship Procedures* (Englewood Cliffs, N.J.: Prentice-Hall, 1964); *Stewardship in Mission,* ed. Winburn T. Thomas (New York: Association Press, 1964); T. A. Kantonen, *Stewardship in Contemporary Life* (New York: Association Press, 1965); Otto Piper, *The Christian Meaning of Money* (New York: Association Press, 1965); *Stewardship Illustrations,* ed. T. K. Thompson (Englewood Cliffs, N.J.: Prentice-Hall, 1965); Martin E. Carlson, *Why People Give* (New York: NCCCUSA Council Press for Stewardship and Benevolence, 1968); Douglas W. Johnson and George W. Cornell, *Punctured Preconceptions: What North American Christians Think about the Church* (New York: Friendship Press, 1972); *Thinking and Preaching Stewardship: An Anthology,* ed. Nordan C. Murphy (New York: NCCCUSA Commission on Stewardship, 1985). Titles published in the 1980s include three by Douglas John Hall: *The Steward, Christian Mission,* and *Imaging God.*

Among the titles projected in the 1960s that never appeared were a stewardship commentary on the Old and New Testaments, *Motivational Aspects in Christian Giving,* and *Stewardship Themes in Great Literature.*

43. J. Reumann, "The Use of *Oikonomia* and Related Terms in Greek Sources to about A.D. 100, as a Background for Patristic Applications" (Ph.D. diss., University of Pennsylvania, 1957). Most of the dissertation was published in *Ekklēsiastikos Pharos* (Athens) 60 (1978) 3-4: 482-597; 61 (1979): 563-603; *Ekklēsia kai Theologia / Church and Theology* (London and Athens) 1 (1980): 368-430; 2 (1981): 591-617; 3 (1982): 115-40.

44. There are exceptions, however; see "The Stewardship Heritage of Southern Baptists" issue of *Baptist History and Heritage* 21 (1986).

45. Hall, *The Steward,* pp. 30-37.

46. See Hall, *The Steward,* pp. 3-5, 53-54, 76-78, 100-113.

47. See Hall, *The Steward,* pp. 69-84.

48. See, e.g., Max L. Stackhouse, *Public Theology and Political Economy: Christian Stewardship in Modern Society* (Grand Rapids: William B. Eerdmans, 1987); and David L. Polk, "The Shalom of Stewardship: Stewardship from a Process Perspective," *Journal of Stewardship* 40 (1988): 42-49.

49. Salstrand, *The Story of Stewardship in the United States of America,* p. 151.

50. Salstrand, *The Story of Stewardship in the United States of America,* pp. 91-146.

51. See Hall, *The Steward,* pp. 36-37, 39, 130-40. "The imperial missionizing assumptions of historic Christianity are no longer really pertinent or even realistic," he writes (p. 137). In *Christian Mission* he forswears mission in the traditional sense on the grounds that the "Constantinian era" has passed, and Christians now have an obligation to respect the

138

rights of other world religions to exist and an obligation to acknowledge "the historically conditioned character of all religious truth" (see pp. 1-8). See also his essay "Mission as a Function of Stewardship," in *Spotlighting Stewardship* (Don Mills, Ont.: United Church of Canada, 1981), pp. 18-44.

52. See Hall, *Christian Mission,* pp. 17-18, 48-54, 59, 63-64. On the theme of Luther's *theologia crucis,* see Hall's earlier book, *Lighten Our Darkness.*

53. Murphy, in *Spotlighting Stewardship,* pp. 9-10; italics mine.

Chapter IV

1. See above, p. 61.

2. Frei, *The Eclipse of the Biblical Narrative: A Study in Eighteenth-and Nineteenth-Century Hermeneutics* (New Haven: Yale University Press, 1974).

3. Lindbeck, *The Nature of Doctrine: Religion and Theology in a Postliberal Age* (Philadelphia: Westminster Press, 1984); and "Confession and Community: An Israelite-like View of the Church," *Christian Century,* 9 May 1990, pp. 492-96.

4. Fackre, *The Christian Story,* vol. 1: *A Narrative Interpretation of Basic Christian Doctrine* (Grand Rapids: William B. Eerdmans, 1984); vol. 2: *Authority: Scripture in the Church and for the World —A Pastoral Systematics* (Grand Rapids: William B. Eerdmans, 1987).

5. Childs, *Introduction to the Old Testament as Scripture* (Philadelphia: Fortress Press, 1978); *The New Testament as Canon: An Introduction* (Philadelphia: Fortress Press, 1984); and *Old Testament Theology in a Canonical Context* (Philadelphia: Fortress Press, 1986).

6. Meeks refers to a number of works as having brought the *oikonomia* concept into prominence as "a new metaphor for God" (*God the Economist: The Doctrine of God and Political Economy* [Minneapolis: Fortress Press, 1989], pp. 2, 186n.4), among them the following: J. Reumann, "The Use of *Oikonomia* and Related Terms in Greek Sources to about A.D. 100, as a Background for Patristic Applications" (Ph.D. diss., University of Pennsylvania, 1957); " 'Stewards of God' — Pre-Christian Religious Application of *oikonomos* in Greek," *Journal of Biblical Literature* 77 (1958): 339-49; and "*Oikonomia* as 'Ethical Accommodation' in the Fathers and Its Pagan Background," in *Studia Patristica III,* ed. F. L. Cross, Texte und Untersuchungen 78 (Berlin: Akademie-Verlag, 1961), pp. 370-79. Meeks writes, "I follow John Reumann's ground-breaking work but, instead of differentiating *oikonomia* and *sdq/dikaiosyne,* I see them as much more closely connected. Righteousness is the work of God's economy" (p. 200n.2). He also cites Reumann, "The 'Righteousness of God' and the 'Economy of God': Two Great Doctrinal Themes Historically Compared," in *Aksum —Thyateira: A*

Festschrift for Archbishop Methodios of Thyateira and Great Britain (London: Thyateira House, 1985), pp. 615-37. For exegetical connections, see J. Reumann, *"Righteousness" in the New Testament: "Justification" in the United States Lutheran–Roman Catholic Dialogue,* with responses by Joseph A. Fitzmyer and Jerome D. Quinn (Philadelphia: Fortress Press, 1982).

7. See C. F. D. Moule, *Man and Nature in the New Testament: Some Reflections on Biblical Ecology,* Facet Books Biblical Series 17 (Philadelphia: Fortress Press, 1967), pp. viii-xvii, 8-14.

8. See, e.g., "Stewardship and the Gospel," *Lutheran Theological Seminary Bulletin* (Gettysburg, Pa.), 70, 4 (Fall 1990), especially E. W. Gritsch, "Gospel and Stewardship: The Perspective of Martin Luther." The thematic question was set as, "Is there an imperative in the gospel?" The essays were therefore compelled to wrestle, because of the way the Lutheran law-gospel dichotomy was interpreted and a simplistic understanding that "imperatives" in the Bible are "law," with whether stewardship is not then law rather than gospel.

9. See Patrides, *The Grand Design of God: The Literary Form of the Christian View of History* (London: Routledge & Kegan Paul, 1972), p. 9. See also his longer monograph *The Phoenix and the Ladder: The Rise and Decline of the Christian View of History* (Berkeley and Los Angeles: University of California Press, 1964).

10. Smith, *Select Discourse* (1660), cited by Patrides in *The Grand Design of God,* p. 70.

11. Edwards, on his *History of the Work of Redemption* (originally sermons in 1739; first American edition, 1786), in a letter of 1757, as cited by Patrides in *The Grand Design of God,* p. 119.

12. See Cullmann, *Christ and Time: The Primitive Christian Conception of Time and History,* rev. ed., trans. Floyd V. Filson (Philadelphia: Westminster Press, 1964); and *Salvation in History,* trans. Sidney G. Sowers et al. (New York: Harper & Row, 1967). For further discussion of Cullmann's views, see Chap. 5 herein.

13. See Wolfhart Pannenberg et al., *Revelation as History* (New York: Macmillan, 1968); Moltmann, *The Experiment Hope,* ed. and trans. M. Douglas Meeks (Philadelphia: Fortress Press, 1975); and Moltmann with H. Cox et al., *The Future of Hope: Theology as Eschatology* (New York: Herder & Herder, 1970).

14. On this, see George W. Coats, "Theology of the Hebrew Bible," in *The Hebrew Bible and Its Modern Interpreters,* ed. D. A. Knight and G. M. Tucker (Philadelphia: Fortress Press, 1985), pp. 239-62. Coats discusses the approaches of Eichrodt, von Rad, Clements, Childs, and others. For proposals concerning "salvation history" in the Old Testament, see Robert Gnuse, *Heilsgeschichte as a Model for Biblical Theology: The Debate concerning the Uniqueness and Significance of Israel's Worldview,*

College Theology Society Studies in Religion 4 (Lanham, Md.: University Press of America, 1989).

15. See Käsemann, "On the Subject of Primitive Christian Apocalyptic," in *New Testament Questions of Today* (Philadelphia: Fortress Press, 1969), p. 137.

16. See Reginald H. Fuller, "New Testament Theology," in *The New Testament and Its Modern Interpreters*, ed. E. J. Epp and G. W. MacRae (Philadelphia: Fortress Press, 1989), pp. 565-84. Neither this volume nor *The Hebrew Bible and Its Modern Interpreters*, both of which were commissioned for the hundredth anniversary of the Society of Biblical Literature, deals with "biblical theology" combining both testaments. For a survey of prospects in light of recent approaches, see *The Promise and Practice of Biblical Theology*, ed. J. Reumann (Minneapolis: Fortress Press, 1991). It is unlikely that a biblical theology will ever be written around the theme of "stewardship" because of the paucity of data, especially in the Old Testament, unless the subject is understood as (1) God's stewardship in both creation and redemption and (2) human stewardship in both creation and the "stewardship of all believers."

Chapter V

1. For treatments of the story of the widow's mite, see J. A. Fitzmyer, *The Gospel according to Luke X–XXIV*, Anchor Bible 28A (Garden City, N.Y.: Doubleday, 1985), pp. 1319-22; and C. S. Mann, *The Gospel according to Mark*, Anchor Bible 27 (Garden City, N.Y.: Doubleday, 1986), pp. 493-96. Instead of reading this story as an example of self-sacrifice for a divine cause, in contrast to the responses Jesus received from all the other groups in Jerusalem mentioned in Mark 12, one can read it as the final and climactic example of incorrect conduct in the face of Jerusalem's doom: the widow is swindled by a corrupt temple cult that will soon be destroyed (Mark 13). Elizabeth Struthers Malbon examines still other readings beyond "financial stewardship" in "The Poor Widow in Mark and Her Poor Rich Readers," *Catholic Biblical Quarterly* 53 (1991): 539-604.

2. See C. K. Barrett, *From First Adam to Last* (New York: Scribner's, 1962), p. 4n.1.

3. See Richardson, *History Sacred and Profane* (Philadelphia: Westminster Press, 1964).

4. See Patrides, *The Grand Design of God: The Literary Form of the Christian View of History* (London: Routledge & Kegan Paul, 1972).

5. See J. Reumann, "Heilsgeschichte in Luke: Some Remarks on Its Background and Comparison with Paul," *Studia Evangelica IV*, ed. F. L. Cross, Texte und Untersuchungen 102 (Berlin: Akademie-Verlag, 1968), pp. 87-88.

6. See M. J. Heinecken, "Erlangen Theology," in the *Twentieth Century Encyclopedia of Religious Knowledge,* vol. 1, ed. L. A. Loetscher (Grand Rapids: Baker Book House, 1955), p. 391.

7. Von Hofmann's major work, *Biblische Hermeneutik* (1860), was translated as *Interpreting the Bible* (Minneapolis: Augsburg, 1959). See also Christian Preus, "The Contemporary Relevance of von Hofmann's Hermeneutical Principles," *Interpretation* 4 (1950): 311-21.

8. Cullmann, *Salvation in History,* trans. Sidney G. Sowers et al. (New York: Harper & Row, 1967).

9. Cullmann, *Christ and Time: The Primitive Christian Conception of Time and History,* rev. ed., trans. Floyd V. Filson (Philadelphia: Westminster Press, 1964). For Cullmann's charts, see the first edition (Philadelphia: Westminster Press, 1949), p. 82; in the revised edition (p. 83), the captions "Before Creation" and "After the Parousia" are dropped. For comments on the changes in the revised edition, see my review in the *Journal of Biblical Literature* 83 (1964): 341.

10. For translations of the Second Vatican Council texts, see *The Documents of Vatican II,* ed. Walter M. Abbott (New York: Association Press, 1966). See also Müller-Fahrenholz, *Heilsgeschichte zwischen Ideologie und Prophetie: Profile und Kritik heilsgeschichtlicher Theorien in der ökumenischen Bewegungen zwischen 1948 und 1968* (Freiburg: Herder, 1974).

11. See Piper, "Heilsgeschichte," in *A Handbook of Christian Theology,* ed. M. Halvorson and A. C. Cohen (Cleveland: World Publishing, 1958), p. 157. Van A. Harvey, *A Handbook of Theological Terms* (New York: Macmillan, 1964), pp. 113-15.

12. See J. Reumann, "*Oikonomia*-Terms in Paul in Comparison with Lucan Heilsgeschichte," *New Testament Studies* 13 (1967-68): 147-67.

13. The Deuteronomist (D), or the Deuteronomist History (DH), preserved in the canonical book of Deuteronomy and in material running through Joshua, Judges, 1–2 Samuel, and 1–2 Kings, assesses leaders not on grounds of prosperity and material success, as a secular historian might, but on the basis of fidelity to Yahweh. There is a theology in D of one God, one people, one land, one cult (see, e.g., Deut. 6:4; 7:7-8; 12:1, 11, 14, 18, 21, 26).

14. The question is especially raised by Brevard Childs's program of "canonical criticism," as presented in *Introduction to the Old Testament as Scripture* (Philadelphia: Fortress Press, 1978); *The New Testament as Canon: An Introduction* (Philadelphia: Fortress Press, 1984); and *Old Testament Theology in a Canonical Context* (Philadelphia: Fortress Press, 1986). In this last volume, Childs treats a variety of topics in the context of collections of books within the canon, such the Pentateuch, histories, the prophets, Psalms, and wisdom literature.

15. For the larger context of the citation of Diodorus Siculus 1.1.3, see p. 21 above.

16. Achtemeier, *The Quest for Unity in the New Testament: A Study in Paul and Acts* (Philadelphia: Fortress Press, 1987), pp. 69-74.

17. Achtemeier, *The Quest for Unity in the New Testament,* p. 73.

18. Papias, *Exegesis of the Lord's Oracles,* as cited by Eusebius in *Ecclesiastical History* 3.39.15.

19. On the contrast, see J. Reumann, "The Use of *Oikonomia* and Related Terms in Greek Sources to about A.D. 100, as a Background for Patristic Applications" (Ph.D. diss., University of Pennsylvania, 1957), pp. 348-83, 590-94, especially n. 141.

20. Conzelmann, *The Theology of St. Luke,* trans. Geoffrey Buswell (1960; repr., Philadelphia: Fortress Press, 1982); Fitzmyer, *The Gospel According to Luke I–IX,* Anchor Bible 28 (Garden City, N.Y.: Doubleday, 1981), pp. 143-258, especially pp. 144, 162-92, and in particular p. 182 on the three phases or eras. See also J. Reumann, "Heilsgeschichte in Luke," pp. 86-115.

21. See S. G. Wilson, *Luke and the Pastoral Epistles* (London: SPCK, 1979).

22. *Clement of Alexandria, The Exhortation to the Greeks, The Rich Man's Salvation,* Loeb Classical Library, trans. G. W. Butterworth (London: Heinemann, 1919), pp. 265-367.

23. See Luke T. Johnson, *Sharing Possessions: Mandate and Symbol of Faith,* Overtures to Biblical Theology 9 (Philadelphia: Fortress Press, 1981); see also his study *The Literary Function of Possessions in Luke-Acts,* Society of Biblical Literature Dissertation Series 39 (Missoula, Mont.: Scholars Press, 1977).

24. See Munck, *Paul and the Salvation of Mankind* (London: SCM Press, 1959). For a sympathetic reaction, see W. D. Davies, "A New View of Paul," in his *Christian Origins and Judaism* (Philadelphia: Westminster Press, 1962), pp. 179-98. And see Stendahl, *Paul among Jews and Gentiles* (Philadelphia: Fortress Press, 1976), pp. 129-32.

25. Among the varied reconstructions of Paul's view of history are the following: C. H. Dodd et al., *Man in God's Design* (Newcastle: Studiorum Novi Testamenti Societas, 1983); Erich Dinkler, "Earliest Christianity," in *The Idea of History in the Ancient Near East,* American Oriental Series 38 (New Haven: Yale University Press, 1955), pp. 181-88; and Ulrich Luz, *Das Geschichtsverständnis bei Paulus,* Beiträge zur Evangelischen Theologie 49 (Munich: Chr. Kaiser Verlag, 1968).

26. Butterfield, *Christianity and History* (New York: Scribner's, 1949), pp. 40-41.

27. This approach has been spelled out, for example, by C. K. Barrett in his book *From First Adam to Last: A Study in Pauline Theology* (New York: Scribner's, 1962).

28. Barrett, *From First Adam to Last,* p. 118; cf. pp. 94-95, 99.

29. See, e.g., Cullmann, *Christ and Time,* pp. 83 (p. 82 in the revised

edition), 188; "Paul's Conical View of History," in W. D. Davies, *Invitation to the New Testament: A Guide to Its Main Witnesses* (Garden City, N.Y.: Doubleday, 1966), pp. 302, 303; and F. R. McCurley and J. Reumann, *Witness of the Word: A Biblical Theology of the Gospel* (Philadelphia: Fortress Press, 1986), p. 345.

30. See Munck, *Paul and the Salvation of Mankind,* especially p. 276; and *Christ and Israel: An Interpretation of Romans 9–11* (Philadelphia: Fortress Press, 1967). See also Stendahl, "The Apostle Paul and the Introspective Conscience of the West," *Harvard Theological Review* 56 (1963): 199-215, reprinted in his *Paul among the Jews and Greeks,* pp. 78-96; cf. pp. 129-32.

31. See Munck, *Paul and the Salvation of Mankind,* pp. 287-308; Keith Nickle, *The Collection: A Study in Paul's Strategy,* SBT 48 (London: SCM Press, 1966).

32. See Betz, *2 Corinthians 8 and 9: A Commentary on Two Administrative Letters of the Apostle Paul,* Hermeneia (Philadelphia: Fortress Press, 1985), pp. 102-26. In dealing with the thesis of 9:6 ("one who sows bountifully will also reap bountifully") and the proofs offered to support it in vv. 7-14, Betz lays bare the crassness of the argument and the frequent classical parallels. The line of argument seems to suggest that the thanksgivings generated to God by the recipients of the gifts of the Corinthians (Achaians) would accrue to the benefit of the givers.

33. On parallels between 2 Cor. 9:14 and Hesiod, Xenophon, and Pliny, see Betz, *2 Corinthians 8 and 9,* pp. 98-100.

34. Greek *isotēs* = "equality"; see Betz, *2 Corinthians 8 and 9,* pp. 67-70.

35. See., e.g., Achtemeier, *Quest for Unity,* p. 60; regarding the fears Paul expresses in Rom. 15:31 and the silence of Acts, see pp. 18, 35, 42, 46.

36. See Raymond E. Brown, *The Semitic Background of the Term "Mystery" in the New Testament,* Facet Books Biblical Series 21 (Philadelphia: Fortress Press, 1968).

37. A striking expression of this love of the earth can be found in a speech made by Chief Noah Seattle of the Duwamish Confederacy when his people were forced to cede tribal lands to white settlers. He spoke eloquently of the sacredness of the soil to his people; even the rocks and dust responded lovingly, he said, because of tribal associations. See Louis Thomas Jones, *Aboriginal American Oratory* (Los Angeles: Southwest Museum, 1965); an excerpt of the speech can be found in Philip H. Pfatteicher's *Festivals and Commemorations* (Minneapolis: Augsburg Press, 1980), pp. 227-28. The text of the speech was set to music by Gregory Youtz for the Washington State Centennial.

Recent historians have cast some doubt on portions of the speech, tracing the ecological lament to a 1971 script used in a Southern Baptist television program. Native Americans of the Southwest, such as the Navajo, provide in their religious worldview and myths of creation undisputed examples of love for the earth by indigenous peoples.

38. Fisher, *A New Climate for Stewardship* (Nashville: Abingdon Press, 1976); and *All the Good Gifts: On Doing Biblical Stewardship* (Minneapolis: Augsburg Press, 1979), pp. 9-10.

39. On this sense of the term, see J. Reumann, "*Oikonomia* as 'Ethical Accommodation' in the Fathers and Its Pagan Background," in *Studia Patristica III,* ed. F. L. Cross, Texte und Untersuchungen 78 (Berlin: Akademie-Verlag, 1961), pp. 370-79.

40. Sittler, *The Care of the Earth and Other University Sermons* (Philadelphia: Fortress Press, 1964).

41. Hatch, *The Influence of Greek Ideas and Usages upon the Christian Church,* 2d ed., ed. A. M. Fairbairn (1901; rpt., New York: Harper Torchbooks, 1957).

42. Concerning Israel and the ancient Near East, see McCurley and Reumann, *Witness of the Word,* pp. 133-51. An exception in Greek literature is Hesiod's *Theogony,* which, however, exhibits ties to Semitic epic transmitted via Asia Minor.

43. See J. Reumann, *Creation and New Creation: The Past, Present, and Future of God's Creative Activity* (Minneapolis: Augsburg Press, 1973), pp. 42-56, especially pp. 44-45; Eduard Lohse, *Colossians and Philemon,* Hermeneia, trans. W. R. Poehlmann and R. J. Karris, ed. H. Koester (Philadelphia: Fortress Press, 1971), pp. 52-55; and Eduard Schweizer, *The Letter to the Colossians: A Commentary,* trans. Andrew Chester (Minneapolis: Augsburg Press, 1982), pp. 57-59, 72, 82-83, 273-77, 298.

44. Hatch, *The Influence of Greek Ideas and Usages upon the Christian Church,* pp. 117-237.

45. Irenaeus, *Adversus Haereses* 1.22; cf. 4.20.

46. Chrysostom, *Oration* 1.37; cf. 42-46.

47. Arrian, *Epicteti Dissertationes* 1.9.4-8. *Epictetus: The Discourses as Reported by Arrian . . . ,* Loeb Classical Library, 2 vols., trans. W. A. Oldfather (London: Heinemann, 1925), 1: 64-67.

48. Arrian, *Epicteti Dissertationes* 2.23.42 (*Epictetus,* 1: 418-19).

49. See McCurley and Reumann, *Witness of the Word,* pp. 236-49, especially p. 240.

50. See McCurley and Reumann, *Witness of the Word,* pp. 215-17, 223-26; and *Creation and New Creation,* pp. 24-42, especially pp. 35-36. The importance of creation as God's work emerged for Christians in the early church's battle against Gnosticism and the contention of that movement that the world had been made by an inferior second god.

51. Carroll Stuhlmueller called the concept "creative redemption" in his monograph *Creative-Redemption in Deutero-Isaiah,* Analecta Biblica 43 (Rome: Biblical Institute, 1970), and, more briefly, in the *Jerome Biblical*

Commentary, ed. R. E. Brown, J. Fitzmyer, and R. Murphy (Englewood Cliffs, N.J.: Prentice-Hall, 1968), 22: 4, 17, and 18; *New Jerome Biblical Commentary* (1990), 21: 5, 17, 18.

52. See McCurley and Reumann, *Witness of the Word,* pp. 210-14.

53. For a translation of the "Hymn to the Aton" by John A. Wilson, see *Ancient Near Eastern Texts relating to the Old Testament,* 3d ed., ed. James B. Pritchard (Princeton: Princeton University Press, 1969), pp. 369-71; and in *The Ancient Near East,* vol. 1: *An Anthology of Texts and Pictures,* ed. James B. Pritchard (Princeton: Princeton University Press, 1958), pp. 226-30.

54. Hall, *The Steward: A Biblical Symbol Come of Age* (New York: Friendship Press, 1982), pp. 76, 120-21.

55. Hall, *The Steward,* p. 120.

56. See Hall, *Christian Mission: The Stewardship of Life in the Kingdom of Death* (New York: Friendship Press, 1985), pp. 18-21, 88-91.

57. Hall, *Christian Mission,* p. 90.

58. Horvath, "Stewards of History," *Journal of Stewardship* 40 (1988): 28-29. See also Horvath's *Being Stewards: Focus on Our Identity as Stewards* (New York: United Church of Christ Stewardship Council, 1987).

59. Rist, "Apocalypticism," in vol. 1 of *The Interpreter's Dictionary of the Bible,* ed. George Arthur Buttrick et al. (Nashville: Abingdon Press, 1962), pp. 157-61.

60. For treatments illustrating these newer trends, see Paul D. Hanson, "Apocalypse, Genre," and "Apocalypticism," in *The Interpreter's Dictionary of the Bible Supplementary Volume,* ed. Keith Crim et al. (Nashville: Abingdon Press, 1976), pp. 27-28, 28-34.

61. Hanson, "Apocalypticism," p. 29.

62. Hanson, "Apocalypticism," p. 29.

63. Hanson, "Apocalypticism," p. 30.

64. Hanson, "Apocalypticism," p. 30.

65. Hanson, "Apocalypticism," p. 31.

66. Paul D. Hanson, *The People Called: The Growth of Community in the Bible* (San Francisco: Harper & Row, 1986), p. 455.

67. See Hall, *The Steward,* pp. 37-38, 135-37; and *Christian Mission,* pp. 9-10, 19-21 (the "minorities" with vision seem increasingly to be outside the mainline churches or any church at all); cf. pp. 92-96. Hall's approach in *Imaging God: Dominion as Stewardship* (Grand Rapids: William B. Eerdmans, 1986) is properly more complex and seems to lay less emphasis on this line of the disenfranchised running through history; see pp. 49-60. Is this, at least in part, because the theme of "the image of God" in human beings was not a feature of apocalyptic thinking? In trying to make God "geocentric," Hall dismisses 1 John 2:15-16 and James 4:4 — passages associating loyalty to God with enmity toward the world — as "isolated texts" (p. 199). But these passages (at least the latter) belong more to a

wisdom than an apocalyptic tradition, and Hall's treatment passes completely over apocalyptic passages, in spite of the emphasis he places (following J. C. Beker) on Paul's "apocalyptic theology" (p. 172).

68. For Hall, this may be the problem issue; see *Imaging God,* pp. 37-42.

69. Ernst Käsemann, among others, has stressed this "future reservation," for example in his 1962 essay "On the Subject of Primitive Christian Apocalyptic," in *New Testament Questions of Today* (Philadelphia: Fortress Press, 1969), pp. 108-37, especially pp. 133-37. For somewhat contrasting views, see two articles in *The Interpreter's Dictionary of the Bible Supplementary Volume* — Elisabeth Schüssler Fiorenza's "Eschatology of the NT," pp. 272-73; and John Hurd's "Paul the Apostle," p. 650. See also J. Christiaan Beker, *Paul the Apostle: The Triumph of God in Life and Thought* (Philadelphia: Fortress Press, 1980), pp. 16-18, 163, 180, and elsewhere. For Cullmann's views, see *Christ and Time: The Primitive Christian Conception of Time and History,* rev. ed., trans. Floyd V. Filson (Philadelphia: Westminster Press, 1964), pp. 84-93, 139-43, 217-21.

70. In Greek *hōs mē,* "as though . . . not." See Hans Conzelmann, *1 Corinthians,* Hermeneia, trans. James W. Leitch, ed. George W. MacRae (Philadelphia: Fortress Press, 1975), pp. 133-34. "Paul's advice is not to withdraw into the safe and unrestricted realms of the inner life," writes Conzelmann, "but to maintain freedom in the midst of involvement" (p. 133). See also Wolfgang Schrage, *The Ethics of the New Testament,* trans. David E. Green (Philadelphia: Fortress Press, 1988), pp. 121, 182, 202, 231.

71. Schrage, *The Ethics of the New Testament,* p. 121.

72. Hanson, "Apocalypticism," p. 33.

73. Schrage, *The Ethics of the New Testament,* pp. 182, 202.

74. See Hanson, "Apocalypticism," pp. 33-34.

75. *The Old Testament Pseudepigrapha,* vol. 1, *Apocalyptic Literature and Testaments,* ed. James H. Charlesworth (Garden City, N.Y.: Doubleday, 1983), pp. 73-74 (trans. E. Isaac).

76. This addition to Mark's Gospel, found in the Freer manuscript, a fifth-century document now in Washington, D.C., is included in *The New Jerusalem Bible* (note 16c) and in the NRSV (note t).

77. On Joachim, see McCurley and Reumann, *Witness of the Word,* pp. 468-69; *Joachim of Fiore in Christian Thought: Essays on the Influence of the Calabrian Prophet,* 2 vols., ed. Delno C. West (New York: Burt Franklin, 1975); Marjorie Reeves, *The Influence of Prophecy in the Later Middle Ages* (Oxford: Clarendon Press, 1969); Delno C. West, *Joachim of Fiore: A Study in Spiritual Perception and History* (Bloomington, Ind.: Indiana University Press, 1983); Bernard McGinn, *The Calabrian Abbot: Joachim of Fiore in the History of Western Thought* (New York: Macmillan, 1985); Delno C. West and Sandra Zimdars-Swartz, *Joachim of Fiore: A*

Study in Spiritual Perception and History (Bloomington, Ind.: University of Indiana Press, 1983); Marjorie Reeves, *Joachim of Fiore and the Prophetic Future* (New York: Harper & Row, 1976); and Marjorie Reeves and Warwick Gould, *Joachim of Fiore and the Myth of the Eternal Evangel in the Nineteenth Century* (New York: Oxford University Press, 1986).

78. The original *Scofield Reference Bible* was published in 1909; a revised edition was published in 1967. The text is that of the King James Version. Scofield's dispensational comments appear in an extensive body of notes.

Chapter VI

1. See, for example, *Confessing the One Faith: An Ecumenical Explication of the Apostolic Faith as It Is Confessed in the Niceno-Constantinopolitan Creed (381),* Faith and Order Paper No. 153 (Geneva: WCC Publications, 1991). In this document, developed by representatives from many churches over a ten-year period, there are frequent references to "the divine economy" (§§16, 73, 140, 236) and "the history of salvation in creation, reconciliation, and eschatological fulfilment" (§15; cf. §§199, 201, 209) as well as to "responsible stewards" of God's creation (§§65, 84-87) and "human stewardship" of the environment.

2. See Gottwald, *The Hebrew Bible: A Socio-Literary Introduction* (Philadelphia: Fortress Press, 1985), pp. 323-25. The time of kings in Israel was characterized by political centralization, social stratification, shifts in land tenure, and the repercussions of foreign trade and diplomacy. For Gottwald's reconstruction of a happier, earlier period, see *The Tribes of Yahweh: A Sociology of the Religion of Liberated Israel, 1250-1050 B.C.E.* (Maryknoll, N.Y.: Orbis Books, 1979).

INDEX OF
─── SCRIPTURE REFERENCES ───

INTERTESTAMENTAL LITERATURE

NEW TESTAMENT

INDEX OF SELECTED
—— SUBJECTS AND PERSONS ——

153